National Ben

THE
POLISHED
PRESENTATION

THE COMPLETE
SPEAKER'S GUIDE

MARY FENSHOLT PERERA

A meticulous, no-nonsense collection of strategies to ensure successful presentations.
—Kirkus Book Reviews

ISBN: 978-0-578-18667-2

Library of Congress Control Number: 2016959022

Cover Photo © 2017 Mary Fensholt Perera. All rights reserved - used with permission.

Oakmont Press
219 West 6th Street
Claremont, CA 91711

PRINTED IN THE UNITED STATES OF AMERICA

"Outstanding! I've looked for a book with this practical approach for my whole career. An easy-to-read and useful approach to fear."

Jeff Hamill, Vice-President, China (Ret.), Starbucks

"This artfully written book is a game changer for professionals in all arenas! Mary peels back the layers of why public speaking is so challenging and offers specific strategies for connecting with any audience to leave a powerful and lasting impression."

Stacy Iverson, President & CEO, Children's Fund, Inc.

"A masterful and well-thought-out guide to overcoming the anxieties and difficulties associated with effective and powerful public speaking. It is perfect for the on-the-go businessperson because the format allows for quick reading and easy reference."

J. Brian Lovely, Esq., General Counsel and Creative Director of Product Development, Sideout Footwear, Volatile Shoewear

"Outstanding. It is readable and well organized. This book will resonate with those who struggle with presentations."

Catherine Morse, Labor and Employment Law Director, Freescale Semiconductor

"An excellent primer for both the experienced and the aspiring public speaker."

Milt Matthews, Board Member of Robert H. Smith School of Business, University of Maryland

"A very simple and complete guide to improving your performance at presentations and public speaking. Learning about the skills necessary to put together an effective presentation is extremely useful."

Tom Joyce, Vice President, Customer and Industry Affairs, The Hershey Company

In loving memory of my father, Edward Clarence,
and with love to my daughter, Emily Caroline

If a child is to keep alive his inborn sense of wonder,
he needs the companionship of at least one adult who can share it,
rediscovering with him the joy, excitement, and mystery of the world we live in.

RACHEL CARSON

CONTENTS

INTRODUCTION

Great speakers were not born that way. No one was born speaking. If you have learned to speak, the hard part is over.

As with any other skill, proficiency in speaking to groups (and the comfort that comes with it) comes with understanding the basics, practicing, evaluating your success, and exploring what might work well next time.

Computer users know this. Singers know this. Golfers know this. Rock climbers know this. Anybody who has ever put together a bike the night before a birthday knows this.

This book will take away the mystery and frustration associated with the anxiety of public speaking. You will learn how normal and healthy this anxiety is, learn to minimize it and manage what might remain so that it becomes invigorating rather than distracting.

This book is not a quick fix for the common anxiety associated with speaking to groups. If a quick fix existed, you and the millions of others who share this anxiety would have already heard about it. You would have already used it. At least, you would have if it were available, affordable, legal, and not harmful to your health. (And I've met some people willing to be flexible on the last three qualifications.)

Part I gives you an evolutionary explanation of your body's natural response to the challenges of public speaking. This understanding helps minimize and manage anxiety.

Part II will help you plan and prepare thoroughly for your presentation.

Part III will prepare you to deliver your presentation with confidence and polish.

While you can choose to read the entire book or turn to a specific topic for just-in-time learning, you will get the best results by first reading Part I thoroughly. Even if you are a very experienced presenter, it will give you new insights and add understanding and meaning to the rest of the book.

PART I

PRESENTATION ANXIETY

1

There's something about most phobias where there's a tiny, tiny corner where you think this really actually could happen.

ROZ CHAST

YOU ARE NOT ALONE

Know Your Enemy

Anxiety about public speaking is so common, it has been awarded phobia status. A phobia is an irrational, abnormal, and persistent fear of a situation or thing despite the awareness and reassurance that it is not dangerous. The fear must be excessive and disproportionate to the situation or thing feared to the extent that it compels the person to avoid it. This avoidance interferes with life—with thoughts, activities, and sleep.

Anxiety about public speaking earned the scientific name "glossophobia" from the Greek terms for "tongue" and "dread." Glossophobia is out of proportion to the logical risk involved. It seems irrational. It causes physical and emotional distress, which, in turn, causes puzzlement, frustration, and embarrassment.

Many people make life and career choices that allow them to avoid speaking to groups. Many go through life convinced that their anxiety is worse than most others feel and resort to explanations such as "I'm just not born to be a speaker," explanations that don't really explain anything at all.

It would be wonderful if there were a simple, single-cause explanation for the common anxiety about presenting to groups. But there is not. It has more than one cause, and this means that explanations that rely on a single cause will always be inadequate and impractical.

As with other types of public speaking, business and professional presentations are challenging for three reasons. Understanding these reasons makes a huge difference in your ability to minimize and manage the almost universal anxiety associated with presentations.

Know Your Enemy

Anxiety is your enemy. You can use the acronym NME (enemy) to remember the three factors that combine to create anxiety.

    N: Nature
    M: Monologue
    E: Exclusion

Understand these factors, take action to deal with each one, and you will vanquish this enemy. Once you let go of simple, single-cause explanations, you are perfectly poised to do this.

1. Nature. The fight-or-flight instinct kicks in when we find ourselves alone, unsheltered, and scrutinized by many others. We have a natural phobia about putting ourselves in a situation which evokes the ancient dangers inherent in violating our most basic survival strategy—safety in numbers.

2. Monologue. We are designed to communicate in dialogue. We are not designed to deliver monologues, and we don't frequently practice them. It is unnatural, and therefore difficult, to extemporize at length in a logical and organized way, and difficult to memorize a quantity of information.

3. Exclusion. Separate from the audience, cut out, some distance from others, we are unable to get the kind of verbal and nonverbal responses and feedback we get when having a conversation. We cannot achieve the feeling of connection we are accustomed to in conversation, and are left to speak in a vacuum.

Any one of these would make us uncomfortable, but combined they create a perfect storm of discomfort and difficulty. Let's look at each factor more closely.

Nature
Looking Back

Come back in time with me. Way back.

You and a small group of clan members are hungry. You leave the safety of the cave to gather food. The sun is high in the sky when, led by vultures, you find a carcass with some meat remaining on the bones. You and your companions are scraping bones and eating when a bird gives a warning cry.

Looking up, you see a pack of giant hyenas approaching. They have been in the brush, watching, and are now moving in unison in your direction. But you are gifted. Evolution has, over millions of years, gifted you with a body rich in resources.

Your body leaps into action even before the conscious mind reacts. Your hypothalamus signals your adrenal gland. By the time you shout a warning to your companions, your adrenal gland is hard at work. Moments later, your heart is pumping three times as fast as before, sending oxygen-rich blood to your muscles. The capillaries under your skin close down; your blood pressure goes up; your eyes dilate. Digestion stops, and even your immune system stops functioning, to allow energy to flow where you most need it. As your group scrambles away, everyone can run faster, jump higher, see better, hear better, even think faster than moments ago.

Person by person, your scattered clan members regroup. As darkness falls, one small boy is still missing.

We evolved in a world almost unimaginably different from this one. The present design of the human body began to evolve approximately 200,000 years ago, and is based on designs that are much, much older.[1] The world has changed but our bodies have not. Now we live in a modern world, but our bodies have not evolved beyond those of the Stone Age. Our bodies are still suited for life in a Stone Age world.

> **Avoidable human misery is more often caused not so much by stupidity as by ignorance, particularly our ignorance about ourselves.**
>
> CARL SAGAN

Anthropologists have found ample evidence that for many hundreds of thousands of years, both early and modern humans were not just hunters and gatherers. We were prey. For the vast majority of our existence on earth, and in the vast majority of places, large carnivores shared the landscapes with us. Within the enormous span of pre-human and then human history, only recently did we dominate nature to the point where we drove large predators—giant hyenas, saber tooth cats, giant short-faced bears, and dire wolves—to extinction. Only very recently did we drive lions, tigers, bears, and wolves to the very brink of extinction. For eons and eons, pre-humans and humans lived and died among these predators. And predators, although terrifying, were not the only dangers.

Today's most common phobias show us how our body is designed to deal with our long history of dangerous environments, with the world our ancestors knew. Here are some fears that make virtually every list of the most common phobias.

Arachnophobia	Fear of spiders
Ophidiophobia	Fear of snakes
Murophobia	Fear of rodents
Claustrophobia	Fear of enclosed spaces
Acrophobia	Fear of heights
Nyctophobia	Fear of the dark
Agoraphobia	Fear of open spaces, of leaving a safe place
Pteromerhanophobia	Fear of flying (height and enclosed space)
Cynophobia	Fear of dogs (wolves, predators)
Glossophobia	Fear of public speaking

Edward O. Wilson is a leader in the fields of evolutionary biology, sociobiology, and conservation. This insight about phobias is from his Pulitzer Prize-winning book *On Human Nature*.

"Consider the phobias. Like many examples of animal learning, they originate most frequently in childhood and are deeply irrational, emotionally colored, and difficult to eradicate. It seems significant that they are most often evoked by snakes, spiders, rats, heights, close spaces and other elements that were potentially dangerous in our ancient environment, but only rarely by modern artifacts such as knives, guns, and electrical outlets. In early human history phobias might have provided the extra margin needed to insure survival: better to crawl away from a cliff, nauseated by fear than to walk its edge absentmindedly."[2]

In the cerebral cortex, the gray matter responsible for thought, memory, reasoning, learning, sensory perception, and voluntary muscle movement evolved relatively recently. The newer part of the brain reasons with logic. Our intellect understands the difference

between leaning over a stair rail or leaning over the edge of a cliff; gazing at a snake through a pane of glass or at our feet; sitting in a movie theater or a starship; jumping from a plane with or without a parachute.

The older parts of our brain cannot make these mental leaps of understanding, and they retain powerful controls over our Stone Age body. The older, deeper structures of our brain evolved much earlier. These parts of the brain have not surrendered the control they have over the rest of our bodies; they maintain homeostasis, keeping our bodies within the range we need for survival. They regulate temperature, moisture content, blood sugar, etc. We can't think ourselves out of shivering when cold, perspiring when hot, or growing hungry or sleepy.

Our nervous system has two major parts. The first, the parasympathetic system, is activated when we are relaxed, and is known as the "rest and digest" part of the nervous system. When active it stimulates blood flow to the brain, extremities, digestive system, and reproductive system. The other part, the sympathetic nervous system, is responsible for the "fight or flight" response. It is activated when we are stressed. It reduces the flow of blood to the brain, extremities, and digestive system in preparation for a perceived survival situation.

Our Stone Age Response to Phobias

Fight or flight refers to the collective physical changes made by the sympathetic nervous system when we experience stress, those designed to get us out of danger.[3] A pounding heart, more rapid breathing, moist palms, dry mouth, shaking, and temporary memory loss are just some of the changes brought on by fight or flight. These changes help us to respond quickly to physical dangers with enough strength and stamina to survive. They prepare us to face the dangers of the ancient world, to fight or flee. But sadly, they make it difficult to accomplish our presentation goals. The newer parts of your brain want to accomplish your goals: to cover the information, to seem knowledgeable, to maintain the interest of the audience, to be understood, to look and sound comfortable and confident, to persuade or motivate or entertain. The older, deeper structures of the brain have no knowledge of this. And they want to be in charge.

In presentation workshops I often offer people this choice: "For the next one to two minutes you can either stand in front of the group and introduce yourself or simply stand in front in silence." Inevitable, nervous laughter comes from the group. Not one person has ever chosen to stand in silence.

A direct stare is typical of the most out-and-out aggression… A professional lecturer takes some time to train himself to look directly at members of his audience… Even though he is in such a dominant position, there are so many of them, all staring (from the safety of their seats) that he experiences a basic and initially uncontrollable fear of them… He has all his intellectual worries about the qualities of his performance and its reception…but the massed threat-stare is an additional and more fundamental hazard for him.

DESMOND MORRIS

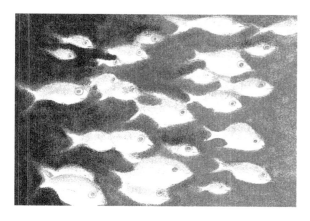

Safety in Numbers

Our ancestors understood on the deepest level that to be alone in the open was dangerous. But to be alone, outnumbered, to face a group or pack all focused on you too often meant you were prey. It was a clear and present danger every bit as terrifying as a poisonous snake or spider, a deep cavern, the edge of a cliff, or the black of night.

Salient object refers to that part of an image that an observer's brain and visual attention focus on. When you give a presentation you are the salient object. Speaking gives you a modern and legitimate reason for becoming the salient object. Without speaking, standing there would be worse! It is more than speaking that causes the anxiety. It is being the salient object.

Our ancestors survived to bequeath to us the deeply rooted abhorrence of being a "salient object" to the eyes of a group of "others." We are all descendants of survivors. This abhorrence is more fundamental than intellectual understanding. It is a survival mechanism, like other phobias, built into the deepest structures of the brain, waiting to be awakened by the first exposure to danger.[4] And this phobia is triggered by the act of standing in front of a group to give a speech.

Drive nature from your door with a pitchfork, and she will return again and again.

HORACE

The "modern" parts of the brain controlling reasoning, logic, and conscious decision making often cannot control our physical response to being the salient object. So, the fear of presenting, triggered by the "dangerous" behavior it requires, is, like other common phobias, a normal and natural part of being human.

What Happens and Why

Changes commonly triggered by phobias, and an explanation of what the body is doing to "help" us follow.

- *Older parts of the brain take over.* This is the key to understanding all the other changes you experience. Survival mechanisms in the midbrain and brain stem take over. The neocortex, the new brain that controls thinking and higher reasoning, shuts down. You now react quickly and experience only the most basic emotions.

- *Deeper and more rapid breathing*. Dilation of the bronchioles and acceleration in the rate of breathing increase the supply of oxygen to the lungs and heart.

- *Pounding heart*. Fight-or-flight chemicals increase the rate and force of contraction of the heart muscle to pump more blood to the muscles for the coming fight or flight.

- *Change in blood flow*. This increases the flow of blood to the brain and major muscles. It also may decrease the blood near the skin surface, lessening the loss of blood if a flesh wound is suffered. This can result in cold hands and feet.

- *Increase in blood pressure*. Restriction of surface blood vessels raises arterial blood pressure. This may help equalize the gravitational drop in blood pressure above the shoulders caused by quickly standing up to prepare for action.

- *Heightened sensitivity*. All your senses are heightened to increase your ability to detect additional signs of danger. You are more sensitive to light, noise, and odors.

- *Dry mouth*. This follows the suspension of "nonessential" physical processes. A temporary stop to digestion allows an increase in the blood—and oxygen—supply to the muscles needed for fight or flight. When digestion stops, the flow of saliva also stops.[5]

- *Increased muscle tension*. Major muscles of arms and legs tense. This prepares the muscles for the strenuous activities—fighting or fleeing—to come.

- *Shaking, shivering, "goose bumps"—the raising of hairs on the body*. This warms the body. It reduces the susceptibility to cold caused by the lessening of blood flow to the surface of the body. The raising of hairs also makes an animal with fur appear larger, stronger, and more threatening to an adversary.[6]

- *Shaking voice*. This is the result of both shaking for warmth and increased muscle tension.

- *Sweaty palms*. In *The Scars of Evolution* author Elaine Morgan offers this explanation. "A monkey's palm sweats…in response to a consciousness of danger. When the monkey makes a decision…to leap from one branch to another, the brain sends out a signal which quickens its heartbeat, sharpens its perceptions, and at the same time dampens the palms to ensure a good grip on the branch it is aiming for. Our own palms sweat in exactly the same way…when we are tense or apprehensive—standing in the wings with stage fright, being introduced to someone we are in awe of, or contemplating a crucial shot in a snooker final."[7]

- *Memory Loss.* The abilities to retrieve memories and form new memories are impaired when the level of cortisol, a hormone produced principally in response to physical or psychological stress and secreted by the adrenal glands, peaks in the brain. This happens about thirty minutes after the stressful event, as when a new mother often forgets the pain of labor as soon as she has successfully given birth.[8] This may be nature's way of helping us deal with extreme stress, or it may be that nature doesn't want us to overthink emergency situations at the expense of acting.

Nature, Mr. Allnut, is what we are put into this world to rise above.

ROSE SAYER (KATHARINE HEPBURN)

As with other phobias, we can manage these reactions when we understand the nature of the changes and work within our nature, not against it. To do so, we need to look at the remaining factors that make up the perfect storm of our NME: monologue and exclusion.

2

**The trouble with her is that she lacks the power
of conversation, but not the power of speech.**
GEORGE BERNARD SHAW

MORE ABOUT THE ENEMY

Monologue and Exclusion

Human nature, complete with phobias, is one part of the perfect storm we experience as anxiety when speaking in front of a group. Let's explore the rest of our NME, monologue and exclusion.

Monologue
The Second Part of the Perfect Storm

As monologues, presentations and speeches violate the normal rules of speaking. Unlike dialogue, monologue is not natural—it is a real stretch. We are hard-wired for dialogue. Dialogue—a conversation between two or more people—is our natural mode of speech.

We have very little opportunity or incentive to become skillful at organizing and delivering monologues. We are rarely asked to do so in our formative years. Instead, we learn not to do monologues. Trying to do a monologue is uncomfortable because it stretches us out of our comfort zone.

As we grow, the importance of listening—, of sharing, of responding to the thoughts and input of others—is continually emphasized. We become dialogue experts. Imagine a cocktail party with groups of three or four people chatting. Now imagine one person speaking for ten minutes without engaging another person in dialogue. Would you invite that person to your next party?

Monologue Overtaxes Memory

Many people assume that if they know the subject matter, they should be able to deliver the content of a presentation from memory. This is not true. To believe that you should be able to deliver a polished monologue because of your knowledge and experience is unrealistic. A monologue is a different kind of undertaking. Monologue is a huge stretch, an unnatural way of speaking, and very different from dialogue. Our memories are simply not designed to remember all the information we plan to present.

Attempting to do so is like making a long list of items to buy for a weeklong wilderness camping trip, then throwing the list away and relying on memory when shopping and packing. You could not even make a list if you didn't already know what to include on it. You know most of what you need when you first make the list because you've been camping before. You add things to the list as they occur to you, or when a fellow camper suggests you bring them. But if you never check the list again, not when shopping and not when packing, you find yourself in the woods without matches.

When planning a presentation, you have a good idea of what you want to cover. You thought about it, researched it, planned it, designed it, built it, demonstrated it, worked with it, tore it apart, and put it back together again. You operate it, understand it, talk about it, write about it, and teach it to others. But delivering a monologue about it to a group is very different.

Emily was preparing for the most important presentation of her life. She was six years old and nearing the successful completion of first grade. Her presentation was scheduled for tomorrow. She would share something with the class. Mrs. Hizon, her teacher, had said it should be "something important to you."

She would share Caroline, the American Girl doll Grandma Dorothy gave her for Christmas.

Her mother asked, "What will you tell the class about Caroline?"

"Well, first I'll tell them that her name used to be Samantha. But I changed it to Caroline because Caroline is my middle name and she looks just like me. She has the same color hair as me, and the exact same color eyes! And that Grandma Dorothy gave her to me for Christmas."

"Will you tell them anything else?"

"I'll tell them that Caroline has her own bed that fits her, and three outfits and that Grandma might get us matching outfits next Christmas. I'll tell them…"

This went on for another minute or so. Emily seemed well prepared.

Caroline went to school with Emily on Thursday morning. Thursday afternoon Emily's mom asked, "How did sharing go this morning?"

"Okay."

"Okay?"

"Yes."

"What did you tell the class?"

"Nothing."

"Nothing?"

"Well, Mom, when I looked at them they were all staring at me. And I started to tell them but then I couldn't."

"Then what happened?"

"Oh! Then they got to ask me questions."

"What kind of questions did they ask?"

"Oh, like where did I get her and what was her name and why do I like her and stuff like that."

"Did you answer the questions?"

"Yes…and then I told them about the matching outfits. And some other stuff, too…"

Humans are excellent learners. But we are not designed for memorizing long strings of words, sentences, and paragraphs. The human memory is predisposed to deliver small chunks of information each time we speak. We almost never decide exactly what to say next until our dialogue partners have responded to us. Emily was easily able to answer the questions of her classmates—to engage in dialogue—even when her planned monologue evaporated. It was Emily's question-and-answer session, a dialogue, which helped her move beyond her own self-consciousness and anxiety. Dialogue helped her supply the information her listeners wanted to hear. Reverting to dialogue helped her relax and remember what she planned to say.

The Third Front of the Perfect Storm

Exclusion

Much of the natural connection between you and the rest of the group was severed when you stood up and faced them. You are excluded, excised, expunged, cut out from the group. Violating the rule of safety in numbers comes at yet another price.

Grounding and Entrainment

Clients often ask me to teach them how to "connect with the audience." They are looking for the feeling of connection that comes from dialogue. They want to know their messages are understood and if the listeners agree or have reservations. They want to know what the audience members think and feel. They want to communicate their own gravity and concern, their own conviction, confidence, and enthusiasm, to the audience.

When you are the salient object, the object of attention and focus, their eyes are on you; their ears are tuned to you. It is impossible for you to do the same with each listener—there are many of them but only one of you.

But there are other things that are different as well. Within a conversation, two other things help you make a connection with others. When you are excised from the group, they are missing. This makes it impossible to connect the same way.

Grounding

Grounding is the first thing missing. Grounding is the process by which we let our dialogue partners know how we have understood their messages, that is, what we think they mean. In conversation, we try to reach a common understanding of the meaning of the messages. We look for evidence from them that our messages have been understood the way we meant them. Grounding is necessary for the coordination of actions because it makes it possible to discover and fix misunderstandings.[9]

We ground our communications in many ways, some verbal, many nonverbal. A raised eyebrow can show skepticism that can be investigated by the partner. Intermittent nodding shows the listener believes she understands the speaker's message. A pertinent question shows the speaker his argument has been followed and allows the questioner to understand the speaker's precise meaning. Paraphrasing a partner's message to check that you understood it correctly is an example of grounding.

Grounding happens most quickly and effectively with face-to-face dialogue. It is easiest when participants take turns speaking and listening, and when they observe each other closely. The need for grounding is a major reason for the sale of airline tickets. It is why so many sales calls are done in person and high-stakes negotiations are done face-to-face. Lack of effective grounding causes miscommunication. When you hear "it was just a communication problem" or "our wires must have gotten crossed" you know there was inadequate grounding between the people involved.

The need for grounding led to the development of the emoticons used so often in emails, and the smiling, frowning, winking face emojis used in texts. Without vocal tones to communicate how we mean something, we resort to a tiny smiling face to show we mean something humorously, a winking face to show we are writing "tongue in cheek," etc.

The need for grounding makes telephone conversations more difficult than face-to-face communications. On the phone, we can't use or observe many of the subtle nonverbal cues that greatly contribute to grounding. Even video conferencing makes it difficult to ground, as more subtle, nonverbal behavior is lost.

The more formal the presentation, the more likely it is it will be communicated as a monologue. By definition, a person delivering a monologue is speaking alone, hearing virtually nothing from the audience. Not their comments. Not their questions. Not their vocal tones. When we deliver a monologue, others are silenced. Silent listeners—sitting, not gesturing, without much in the way of facial expression—give us little opportunity to ground our message. When subtle changes occur we are likely to miss them, as we can't observe everyone in the audience at every moment. In many ways we are "working in the dark."

So how can we possibly connect? The lack of grounding makes it difficult to know how we're doing. "Are they getting anything out of this?" we ask ourselves. "I wish I knew what they were thinking." "Should I do anything differently?" If we don't have the freedom of protocol or the skill to make the presentation interactive, we will not know.

Entrainment

Entrainment is the second thing missing when we are excised from the group. A simple example of entrainment is the person who taps his toe or bobs his head in time to music.

Every living human body is a physically oscillating system. We vibrate. The rhythms of our breathing, of our heartbeat, of our brainwaves are just a few of the vibrations we generate. Each of us is a mass of vibrations. We really do give off "vibes." Every living human does.

Resonance is the effect of one vibration on another. To resonate is to "re-sound." Sound waves can shift frequency. When in dialogue with others we begin to influence and be influenced by their vibrations. Given time, we fall into a simple temporal relationship with each other; we tend to perform motions in the same amount of time or a simple integer ratio of time, such as half time or double time. Our vibrations and those of another.

This is an important part of feeling connected. In dialogue, people begin to entrain, to resonate with each other. We might slow our rate of speech a bit to match that of another. Subtle changes may occur in the size and speed of gestures we use. This process is often referred to as a dance. The subtle dance of entrainment is well documented.[10] We begin to synchronize vibrations, to influence and be influenced by the vibrations of others. In a very real sense, we begin to "tune in" to each other. We resonate.

Two attempts at entrainment with a large group include a musician encouraging the crowd to clap along with the music or cheerleaders leading fans in the stands in a repetitive chant. But both require that members of the crowd join in making a great deal of noise, and both die out quickly.

Can you entrain with a group when excluded?

It is impossible for a lone speaker to "tune in" to listeners this way when excised from the group. If one person is a mass of vibrations, the vibrations from ten people are cacophony. The vibrations of fifty people, or five hundred people, now farther from us, will likely have trouble reaching us at all. If they do, this mass of vibrations will hit our own vibrations more like a buzz or like white noise. We won't be able to entrain with it. The feeling will never be the same as talking to an individual.

For a presenter, exclusion from the group makes grounding and entrainment, two vital components of achieving the feeling of connection, impossible.

The Perfect Storm

So the enemy of the presenter is the perfect storm of these three elements:

1. *Nature* makes the fight-or-flight response a natural and normal occurrence, leading to anxiety and physical discomfort.

2. *Monologue* requires that we abandon the comfort of dialogue. We must tax our memories, organize our thoughts, and speak in unnatural ways, thus increasing our anxiety and discomfort.

3. *Exclusion* from the group makes it impossible for us to feel the kind of connections we do in dialogue, and makes our anxiety and discomfort even more acute.

Knowledge Is Power

If you don't understand this, and know how to reduce and manage the natural challenges, presenting will be difficult. Worse, you will likely explain the anxiety in ways that are both false and destructive. You may attribute them to past experience, skill set, natural ability, personality, or character, none of which are true.

When you do understand why presenting is, by nature, challenging, and when you know how to manage and overcome these challenges, it becomes fun and rewarding. This chapter has explained the perfect storm; how nature, monologue, and exclusion combine and interact to create challenges. The next chapters will give you specific recommendations and tools to overcome these challenges so you can have fun and experience the rewards.

There are many versions of the following story. John Shea tells the version I like best in his book *Starlight*[11] and credits it to the storyteller Bob Wilhelm. I have condensed it here, adding a few final details from the version found in *St. Francis of Assisi: A Biography* by Omer Englebert.[12]

Francis and the Wolf

In thirteenth-century Italy the small city of Gubbio was nestled in the foothills of a great mountain. It was a beautiful city full of fountains, churches, and sculptures. The people of Gubbio were justifiably proud.

One night, out of the deep and dark woods surrounding Gubbio, a shadow emerged. It prowled the streets of the city until it came on someone walking alone. Then it pounced.

In the morning the people of Gubbio discovered a mangled and gnawed body. In anger and shock they asked, "How could this happen in Gubbio?" The people agreed: it must have been the work of a stranger passing through. That night the people locked their doors and stayed inside. All except for one woman.

In the morning her body was found, mangled and gnawed. The people of Gubbio again agreed it could only be the work of a stranger. But then an old woman spoke.

"I could not sleep. From my window I saw a wolf. A large gray wolf with blood dripping from his mouth!"

Two men, eager to be admired, decided to rid the town of the wolf. That night, heavily armed, they took to the streets to wait for the wolf. In the morning what remained of their bodies was found. Now terrified, the people of Gubbio gathered and shouted demands that the wolf be found and dealt with. But how?

Finally a small girl spoke of a holy man in a neighboring city. This man could speak to animals. An old man said he, too, had heard of the holy man. Could it hurt to try?

The delegation formed to fetch Francis received many suggestions from the people of Gubbio.

"Tell him to tell the wolf to honor the commandment 'Thou shalt not kill.'"

"No, appeal to the good in him. Tell him to love his neighbor!"

"A wolf is a wolf! He cannot change! Tell him to go to Perugia. They deserve a wolf! Or to Spoletta! In Spoletta they wouldn't even know he was there!"

When the delegation reached Francis, the members told him of the horror in Gubbio and begged him to come. St. Francis listened, told them he would see what he could do, and asked them to go home.

The next morning the people of Gubbio woke to find Francis standing near the fountain at the center of town. As a crowd gathered, the people demanded to know what St. Francis had told the wolf to do. He waited, and when they became quiet he said, "My good people of Gubbio, the answer is very simple. You must feed your wolf." Then he walked away and returned to his own city.

The people shouted, "What does he mean? This is not our wolf! We did not ask the wolf to come! How can he say, 'You must feed your wolf'?"

But that night, a platter of food was offered to the wolf. The food was taken, and the killing stopped. The wolf was fed the next night and the next until every man, woman, and child had fed the wolf. The town continued to care for the wolf, and the wolf came and went freely, bothering no one. When it died of old age, the townspeople grieved, for they had become attached to it.

Our NME Is Our Wolf

Our NME, our enemy, our anxiety and fear, is our "wolf." Like the wolf of Gubbio, it can appear suddenly and refuse to leave. Denying the fear, or hoping it will disappear, is as ineffective as hoping the wolf is just passing through, ordering the wolf to obey the Commandments, or demanding that it move to Perugia. Like the people of Gubbio, we must learn to live with our wolf. When we do, we have taken the first, most important step to reducing anxiety and increasing our confidence.

A single sunbeam is enough to drive away many shadows.

FRANCIS OF ASSISI

But this does not mean accepting it and throwing up our hands. It does mean that we understand each of the three reasons that combine to stir up the perfect storm of anxiety, and take actions to compensate for each one.

Understanding and accepting our human nature brings less anxiety and more confidence. When we understand the body's natural response to public speaking we can begin to use the lessons of dialogue learning to overcome it.

Just as the townspeople of Gubbio were unwilling to accept that the wolf was "their" wolf, many people find it hard to accept that the anxiety they feel is a normal, natural response to the challenge of making a presentation. Even more difficult to accept is that most of us will never be able to convince our wolf to move to another town. But like the people of Gubbio, we can learn to understand the nature of our NME, our wolf, and learn to tame it.

Managing Nerves

Understanding that anxiety is natural and normal is one part of minimizing it.

There are many other things you can do before and during your presentation to help. Each chapter in Parts II and III will give you specific tips, explanations, and examples of preparing so that you find it easier to create the look and feel of dialogue and so feel relaxed and completely prepared. Here are a few basics that will help as well.

In the Days Before Your Presentation

Visit the Venue

Many people have difficulty sleeping their first night in a hotel. The body is reluctant to let down its guard completely in a strange place, a natural Stone Age protective mechanism that makes it hard to relax as we would in our own bedroom. The home team advantage in sports is another example of this. Sport professionals know this, and often walk the opponent's home field or court before the event.

This applies to speaking as well as sleeping and sport competitions. Do whatever you can to "own" the space. Walk the room, walk the stage, note where the doors are (Stone Age bodies want to know). Touch the walls, the lectern, and tables and chairs. Find and use the light switches.

Rehearse in the Presentation Room

Even an abbreviated rehearsal is better than a visit alone. Make sure all needed equipment is available and working well. The presentation will feel more comfortable the second time around.

Get Enough Rest

Over the several days (and nights) before your presentation, get plenty of sleep. For at least three hours before bed avoid any stimulants—nicotine, coffee, tea, and soft drinks with caffeine. Avoid after-dinner drinks. Alcohol can help you fall asleep, but the sleep you get will be light and fragmented, not restorative.[13] Sleep allows your brain and body to complete processing the input from your day, recharge your battery, and reboot your applications.

Eat Smart

Refined sugar, such as that in soft drinks, candy, ice cream, pastries, and desserts, and simple starches like white flour can give you problems as your level of blood sugar changes rapidly. These may include mood swings, anxiety, light-headedness, weakness, trembling, and palpitations and exacerbate the normal stress of presenting. Substitute fresh fruit for sweets and replace simple starches with complex carbohydrates such as whole grain breads, vegetables, and brown rice.[14]

Exercise

Get plenty of exercise. Two days before your presentation is not the time to overdo and become stiff, sore, exhausted, or injured. But gentle exercise, especially a combination of aerobic, strength, and flexibility training, will help you minimize your feelings of anxiety. Exercise reduces your skeletal muscle tension and increases the rate of metabolism of excess adrenaline in your body, thus reducing the intensity and duration of the fight-or-flight response. Exercise increases the flow of oxygen to the brain, increasing alertness and concentration. Exercise also stimulates the production of endorphins, natural substances that increase your sense of well-being and confidence.[15]

The Day of Your Presentation

Get There Early

This matters a great deal to your Stone Age body and brain. Anxieties about finding the venue, being late, and not knowing if the room will be appropriate and appropriately prepared are all unsettling. The need to scramble once you arrive only adds to the stress hormones in your bloodstream and makes concentration and focus more difficult to achieve. The Polished Presentation Checklist (Chapter 15) will give you specifics on how to make sure you arrive with plenty of time to spare.

Mingle With the Audience

Before your presentation, greet and introduce yourself to members of the audience as they arrive. Chat with them. Learn about them: their reasons for coming, their challenges and concerns. Confirm what you assumed and discover what you didn't know. Learn their names so you can present to acquaintances rather than strangers. You can tailor your presentation based on what you learned and use examples or references most meaningful to the audience. You can much more easily create the look and feel of dialogue.

Intellectual and Emotional Strategies

Understanding and practicing techniques that reduce intellectual and emotional anxiety will allow you to start with confidence, think more quickly, and focus more effectively on your listeners. Try a suggestion below as you wait to begin.

Concentrate on a simple mental task. Mentally drive a familiar route, naming each street and visualizing the buildings you pass. Try to remember all the words to a song or poem. Add up all the costs of a project.

Remember a success. Recall and celebrate a positive experience. Visualize it happening. Recall the feelings. Feel the satisfaction, joy, and pride.

Use coping self-statements. Tell yourself things that are both positive and true:

"My body is reacting as it is designed to."
"Anxiety is normal. I will do well even if I am uncomfortable."
"I am well prepared."
"My goal is to share this information with people who need it."
"Breathing deeply helps me relax."

Use simple externalization. Consciously and deliberately focus on something external. Observe and silently describe the people around you. Note their physical appearance, items of clothing, colors, and fabrics, in as much detail as you can. Do the same for their physical behavior. Do they move slowly or quickly? How would you describe various facial expressions and tones of voice? Listen closely. Note as many sounds as you can: the hum of the ventilation system, the ticking of a clock, footsteps, the rustle of clothing, conversations going on around you, sounds from the adjoining room.

Feel the temperature and texture of your clothing. Notice the temperature of your chair, table, or desk. Feel the texture of papers you hold.

Physical Strategies

Breathing well is one of the most powerful relaxation techniques. It will relax your muscles, energize your entire body, and oxygenate your brain for peak performance. Use the technique below frequently in your daily life. Remember to use it just before you begin your presentation.

Diaphragmatic Breathing

Diaphragmatic breathing—breathing more slowly and deeply than we do when anxious—can reduce many of the physical symptoms of anxiety in two ways. First, slower, deeper breathing can help reverse two reactions to the fight-or-flight response: increased rate of respiration and tightness in the muscles of the upper body, especially the chest and throat.

Second, deeper breathing reduces the tendency to hyperventilate, which causes symptoms very similar to the fight-or-flight response. This breathing exercise can help you to relax. You will probably notice the effect quickly, but try to allow enough time to continue the exercise for at least several minutes.

Step 1. Place one hand lightly on your abdomen. Inhale slowly through your nose. This warms and moistens the air fully before it enters your lungs. Inhale until you feel your hand rise slightly as the abdomen slowly expands. Count to four or five. You may feel your chest move slightly, but your shoulders and neck should remain relaxed. Inhale until you feel comfortably "full."

Step 2. Remaining quiet and still, hold your breath for several seconds. You may want to visualize the oxygen flowing to all parts of your body or visualize any pleasant and relaxing scene. Hold your breath only as long as you are comfortable doing so.

Step 3. Exhale slowly and gently through your mouth or nose until your lungs feel comfortably empty. Do not force or blow the air out. Let your muscles relax as you exhale. Count the length of your exhale. Matching the duration of the exhale to your inhale will create a balanced and calming breath.

Step 4. Take two or three "regular" breaths. Allow your body to determine the speed, depth, and rhythm of these breaths. As you continue with this exercise, let your body decide what is comfortable.

Step 5. Continue this cycle of one slow, counted, diaphragmatic breath and two or three regular breaths for several minutes.

This diaphragmatic breathing exercise is most effective when you are familiar and comfortable with it. Practicing it daily can give you this comfort. The benefits of deep breathing will help you manage daily stress.

Movement

Look for ways to engage in mild exercise before, and even during, your presentation. The information on "spark" skills in Chapter 14 will give you specifics on using your body effectively during your presentation. These specific instructions will help you both look and feel more relaxed and confident.

Try the following suggestions for anxiety-reducing physical activity just before your presentation.

- Go for a brisk walk. Even a five-minute walk will help you relax, loosen your muscles to relieve tension, and give you a circulation boost that will increase the flow of oxygen and help you think clearly. The rhythm of brisk walking, so soothing to infants that the rocking chair was invented to mimic it, may do a great deal to relax and soothe you when you need it.[16]

- Exercise in place. Stretching, bending, arm circles, or other simple exercises will give you many of the same benefits even when you can't go for a walk.

- Flex your muscles. When even stretching and bending are not possible (for example, when seated on the stage for some time before your turn to speak), tighten and then release your muscles repetitively while you breathe slowly and deeply. You will get many of the benefits of more vigorous movement.

- Stand up early. I often hear people say, "The first couple of minutes of a presentation are always the worst!" Standing up several minutes before you begin speaking can be a big help. When we first rise to a standing position, blood drains from the upper body, including the heart and brain. It takes the body several minutes to readjust the blood volume. Meanwhile, the brain has less oxygen than it needs for peak performance. Just when you need to think most clearly—to step on the gas and fire on all cylinders—you will be operating with too little fuel. Standing up several minutes before you begin speaking allows your body to readjust before you begin your presentation. See the information in Chapter 9 on using posture to help yourself relax and breathe freely.

- Engage in repetitive activity. Count ceiling or floor tiles. Count the number of chairs you see. Tap your fingers or your foot rhythmically. Fold and unfold a piece of paper in a complex pattern. Focusing on something other than your anxiety, and the rhythm you establish, can soothe.

Power Pose

In her popular TED talk, "Your Body Language Shapes Who You Are," social psychologist Dr. Amy Cuddy explains how the body language one uses impacts observers' assumptions, and, often more importantly, one's sense of self. She demonstrates and explains how standing in a position of confidence and power—upright, balanced, with feet at upper hip distance apart and hands on hips (the classic Wonder Woman pose)—can affect our brain. When held for just two minutes, this posture can significantly increase testosterone, thus increasing our sense of confidence, and reduce cortisol, thus lowering our own level of stress. [17]

Medication

Understanding the reason for symptoms, accepting them, and preparing well so you can create an atmosphere of dialogue with your audience are usually the best ways to reduce and manage anxiety. Some people, however, choose to use a beta-blocker to reduce the physical symptoms of anxiety. A small dose before a speech can reduce the flow of adrenaline that occurs with anxiety. [18]

The effects of beta-blockers are not always positive. Some users report a loss of energy. Other possible side effects include dizziness, light-headedness, and allergic reactions. [19] Beta-blockers can be dangerous for people with asthma, diabetes, and certain other allergies. If you do decide to use a beta-blocker, discuss it with your doctor. Ask about trying a test dose before the day of your presentation to make sure you have no negative side effects.

Summary

The fear of presenting, like other common phobias, is part of human nature. It is a normal and natural part of what we are as humans. It is present in differing degrees in different people. Like phobias such as the fear of snakes, heights, and the dark, it helped protect us in our ancient environments. The fear we feel when finding ourselves separated from the safety of our group—the salient object—evokes a natural and deeply rooted fear: the fear of becoming prey.

The human body, the product of millions of years of evolution in physically dangerous environments, is designed to respond defensively to the perception of danger. Although the logical human brain may realize that public speaking presents no real physical danger, the human body retains an innate warning system. This system triggers the fight-or-flight response. The body doesn't distinguish between intellectual challenges, emotional challenges, or physical challenges. Instead, it responds in the only way it knows how—with a flood of hormones that increase our body's ability to deal with physical dangers.

To ignore or deny the reality of this response is not productive. When we understand, accept, and learn to work with the natural responses of our bodies, not against them we experience reduced anxiety and increased confidence. To get this done, we must first accept that fear and anxiety associated with public speaking are normal and healthy. Then, rather than use our energy in frustration or denial, we can invest it in mastering new skills that will further increase our confidence and comfort. They may even lead to a real enjoyment of public speaking.

Leveraging the Lessons of Dialogue

You can learn to deliver a polished presentation by applying many of the same behaviors and techniques you already do when in dialogue and using the behaviors characteristic of dialogue to make your presentations more genuine, natural, and comfortable. You will learn many ways to incorporate the natural rhythms of dialogue into the delivery of your content. You will learn how to enter into genuine dialogue with members of your audience without losing control of your presentation.

Many tools are ready and waiting to help you. The remaining chapters of this book will explain these tools and teach you to use them to your advantage. None of them are complex or, with just a bit of practice, especially difficult to use. You already use many of them in everyday dialogue, and will learn to use them when delivering a monologue. The keys to your success will be accepting that monologues are challenging in nature and being willing to work with whatever tools you choose to help you get the job done.

Now that you understand the nature of presentation anxiety, you can work within your nature as a human being to move beyond it. This will give you confidence and a sense of control.

The rest of this book will take you through the things you need to know before, during, and after a presentation. Part II will prepare you to present. Part III will help you deliver your presentation and answer questions. Everything you learn will help you to deliver a polished presentation, one you can be proud of.

Technology changes all the time; human nature, hardly ever.

EVGENY MOROZOV

The instructions and tips that follow will help you work within the framework nature provides. Both you and your listeners benefit when you harness the power of dialogue to make your presentations more natural, more comfortable, more impactful, and more memorable.

PART II

DESIGNING YOUR PRESENTATION

3

There are two types of people.
Those who come into a room and say, "Well, here I am!"
and those who come in and say, "Ah, there you are."
FREDERICK L. COLLINS

IT'S ALL ABOUT THEM

Reach Your Audience, Then Your Goals

Your presentation is scheduled. Nothing will increase your comfort level more than getting started early. Yet, how to get started can be a puzzle. The chapters in this part of the book will complete this puzzle.

The very first step is to answer these two questions:

1. What do you want?

2. What do your listeners want?

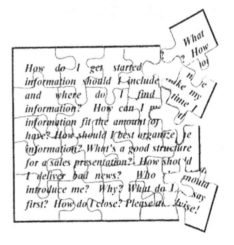

Think hard about both. Focusing on just one of these questions will not give you the same opportunity for success.

What Do You Want?

You will have several goals. Some may be personal, some professional. This contributes to your challenge. But awareness of all your goals is one key to designing and delivering a great presentation. How many of these goals do you have?

Build rapport and trust
Inform the audience
Educate the audience
Persuade the audience
Sell a product or service
Entertain the audience
Create new relationships
Expand a relationship
Improve a relationship
Preserve a relationship
Control a crisis
Contain damage
Demonstrate knowledge
Learn from the audience
Change the listeners' minds
Help the listeners agree
Increase my visibility
Practice my speaking skills
Enjoy myself
Survive

Most likely your goals are interdependent. For example, could you expand a relationship or change listeners' minds without also building trust? Could you persuade them or change their minds without also educating them? To achieve your goals, you must know enough about your listeners to tailor your content and delivery to them.

Who Are They?

Four things to consider in thinking about your audience are power, credibility, psychographics, and demographics.

1. Power. What is the power relationship between you and your audience? If there is a pending decision—a sale to be made, agreement to be reached, or votes to win or lose—who has decision-making power? Who influences the decision?

2. Credibility. How much credibility do you have with the audience? How much do they have with you? What is their opinion of your competence, your character, your confidence, and your intentions? What is your opinion of theirs? How do they perceive each other?

3. Psychographics. How do you relate to the audience in terms of attitudes, values, belief systems, and ideologies? How do they relate to each other? What do they value? Do you share those values? Where might you differ from the audience? How fundamental are these differences? Should you attempt to overcome them or work within them? Can you do either?

4. Demographics. How do you relate to the audience in terms of age, gender, education, socioeconomics, and political beliefs? What cultural differences or language differences do you need to consider? Do members of the audience differ on these factors?

Consider the following more specific questions about your listeners. Answering these questions will help you identify and describe your listeners in detail. With this knowledge and understanding you can tailor your information to them. This will help alleviate content concerns, increase rapport, enhance your credibility, and help you be most persuasive.

- Who will attend? What are their names? Job titles? Job responsibilities?

- Who makes the decisions? What decision-making power do they have?

- Who influences the decisions? What power of influence do they have?

- How important is the topic to your audience? How much do they care?

- What emotions do they have around this topic or issue? Why?

- What do they believe they need? What limitations do they have?

- What problems do they need to solve? What challenges do they have?

- What are their attitudes about your subject? Your organization? You?

- What do they know? What concepts will you need to explain?

- How familiar are they with the issues? How much technical understanding do they have? What terms should be used, defined, or avoided?

- What are their costs in money, time, effort, and risk? Can they pay? Will they?

- Does your audience have any unusual needs?

- Do you need to take their history into account?

- Are some topics taboo?

- What are their ages? Genders? Education level? Cultural backgrounds? Do these factors matter?

Make Educated Guesses

Jot down your answers. Sometimes you will have specific information. Sometimes you can make an educated guess. Your answers are likely to come from a wide variety of sources. These may include previous contact with audience members, research you have done, your previous experience, and your knowledge of the industry. Most likely you were asked to speak because you are knowledgeable.

> People will sit up and take notice of you if you will sit up and take notice of what makes them sit up and take notice.
>
> FRANK ROMER

Fill in the Blanks

You can learn more about your intended audience in many ways. If you will speak at a conference, learn what kind of information is gathered as part of the attendance reservation process. You can discover organizations, job titles, geographic information, and much more this way. If you will speak as a technical expert as part of a sales effort, learn about the situation and the client from the account manager or event host. Depending on the nature of your talk and your audience, one or more of the following options can help you learn what you need to be most effective:

- Ask people who plan to attend: in person, by phone, email, or text message.

- Visit the Web site of the organization you will address.

- Read the corporate report of the company you will speak to.

- Read industry publications.

- Search online for press coverage.

- Send an email survey to those who will attend.

- Include a survey as part of registration to attend.

- Chat with audience members as they arrive for your presentation.

- Take a "show of hands" survey at the beginning of or during your presentation.

Types of Business Listeners

When you have answered the above questions, added your educated guesses, and done any needed research, you will often be able to identify your listeners as belonging to one or more of the following groups: executives, experts, technicians, customers, suppliers, or end users. Understanding the responsibilities, interests, and needs of these types is another great way to make sure you choose the right content, level of detail, and delivery methods.

Executives

Executives make business, financial, legal, administrative, governmental, and political decisions. They are concerned with shareholder value and market share. They decide whether to approve, fund, build, and market new products and programs. They decide whether to continue, expand, or shrink ongoing efforts. They set overall strategy and long-term goals.

Experts

Experts know their company's and/or industry's products and services extremely well. They designed them (or similar products or services), they tested them, and they understand their history, strengths, weaknesses, and opportunities for improvement. They understand the theories and issues related to these products and services. They often have advanced degrees and operate in research and development or academic areas of business or government. They are especially appreciative of elegance of design. Experts generally present information to other experts, to technicians, and to executives.

Technicians

Technicians build, operate, administrate, maintain, and repair the products that the experts theorize about, design, modify, and improve. They have detailed knowledge and extensive experience. Their knowledge is practical.

Customers

Customers purchase or recommend the purchase of your products and/or services. They may be executives, experts, technicians, or end users, and, occasionally, suppliers. In large organizations your customers are most often executives and experts in other organizations.

End users

End users of your product, service, or idea are typically non-specialists. Their interests are usually highly practical—they want to use the product, service, or idea to accomplish their tasks. They have immediate needs and may think shorter term. They may have very little technical knowledge. Non-specialists are least likely to understand what experts and technicians are saying. Demonstrations and hands-on time are often highly effective with non-specialists.

Suppliers

Suppliers provide products or services that contribute to other organizations' ability to satisfy their own customers and employees. They may be executives, specialists, or technicians, or in marketing and sales positions.

If all the members of your audience have similar needs and expectations, knowing what these are may be quite simple. But often, different audience members have different wants, needs, knowledge levels, and opinions. What do you do if members don't all have the same wants and needs?

Plan for a Diverse Audience

Speaking to an audience with members who have identical backgrounds and interests is a luxury in today's world. Most audiences have members with a variety of educational backgrounds, training, experience, specialties, and expertise. Their interests may be very different, and their ability to understand specialized information may vary widely.

There is no way to please all of the people all of the time. It is unlikely you will be able to deliver the precise content, level of detail, and tone that will completely satisfy everyone. But happily, most listeners understand and expect this diversity in the audience. They will understand your challenge—and will appreciate your awareness of it—if you follow these recommendations.

Acknowledge the Situation

When you start, tell the audience that you are aware of the differences in background and interest. You might say something like this: "I know that some of you have been using this software since the first release and will be especially interested in the new features. I understand that some of you will soon be implementing this system for the first time and will want a general understanding of the functions and benefits we offer."

When you acknowledge the diversity, you accomplish two objectives. First, you demonstrate that you understand the audience, are aware of their goals, and care enough to want to give them all something of value. Second, you increase each member's awareness that others' goals may be different from their own. This goes a long way in establishing your credibility. It helps everyone understand and accept your next step.

Share Your Presentation Strategy

Present your strategy for dealing with this situation. Often, the best approach is to target the level of detail to the less technical or least specialized portion of your audience. Another option is to vary the amount of specialized or detailed information at different times. But no matter what your strategy is, share it with your audience.

> **Much unhappiness has come into the world because of bewilderment and things left unsaid.**
>
> FYODOR DOSTOYEVSKY

Simplify or Reduce the Level of Detail

If you plan to simplify the information, tell the audience you have made this choice. Then let them know how you will provide more in-depth or technical information if they want it. Times and methods you can use to provide details and specialized information include

- During the question-and-answer session

- After the presentation

- In handouts or supplementary material

- By phone or email

- On your Web site

- From customer service representatives

- From technical support representatives

- At your trade-show booth

- At an on-site demonstration

Vary the Amount of Specialized Information

Another option is to acknowledge that you will vary the amount of specialized information during your presentation. Ask the audience to understand and bear with you when you do so. Just before you shift from less to more specialized information, let your audience know you are doing so, and give them an estimate of how long it will take. The less specialized audience members will be extremely grateful for any information about how long a section of your presentation will take. You might say something like this: "Now let's cover the specifics of the research design and the statistical tools used. This will take about three minutes. Then we will move right into our findings and recommendations."

Use Language the General Audience Will Understand

Specialized language has several uses. It allows for precision in meaning, but it is also a powerful tool that will unite or divide your audience. This is especially true when the audience has diverse backgrounds.

When the entire group understands the specialized language, it creates a feeling of group cohesiveness. This comes from the unspoken awareness that "we are all enough alike to understand what that means." But it can also mystify and exclude. Lawyers are legendary for using unnecessarily complex language to mystify their activities. This creates a separation between themselves and their clients and helps establish and preserve an aura of indispensable expertise. As experts, they increase their ability to operate with less interference from clients.

And they can command high fees.

The key to using specialized language effectively is to understand it can unite or divide your audience. Meaning and understanding are lost if members of the audience aren't familiar with the specialized language, the acronyms, or the buzzwords used by a speaker. The listeners who don't understand are immediately separated, intellectually and emotionally, from the listeners who do.

Just as importantly, the inability to understand specialized language separates the listeners from the speaker. For a speaker hoping to reach both the minds and hearts of listeners, the overuse of specialized language can create a wall that can't be scaled. So use acronyms and specialized language consciously and sparingly. Instead of saying, "The primary care practitioner apprised the interested party that the subject of recent ministrations had experienced the ultimate irreversible and permanent negative health-care outcome," say, "The doctor said the patient died."

When you use specialized language, make it as understandable as possible to the general audience. If you must use acronyms, tell the audience what they mean and remind them of the meaning at least once.

Make It Interesting and Understandable

Use examples, analogies, anecdotes, and stories to increase interest and understanding. But choose wisely. Simple examples may not be useful to experts, and highly technical ones will go over the heads of non-specialist users and listeners. An analogy helps present new or complex information by comparing it to something already known and understood. A good anecdote or story will help listeners remember your information and share it with others later. Read the lessons on developing and using analogies and stories in Chapter 5 for more information on how to use these tools well. Putting this to use will make a tremendous difference in how the less specialized members of your audience respond to your presentation and to you.

Encourage Questions During Your Presentation

Another good way to handle mixed audiences is to have frequent, brief question-and-answer sessions. If time and protocol allow, invite your audience to ask questions at any time. Let them know how to get your attention (e.g., raising their hands) or, after each major topic, stop and ask, "What questions do you have so far?"

The questions you get will give you information about the ability of the audience to understand your information as well as their interests and concerns. The answers will give less technical people a better understanding of the issues and help prepare them for the next topic. Also, answering questions is a great way to move from monologue to dialogue. Many speakers report that a brief question-and-answer session early in the presentation creates a cooperative atmosphere and relaxes them tremendously.

Thoroughly researching and analyzing your audience is an important first step in preparing your presentation. If it seems to go slowly, remember this: Presentations should be like painting your living room. Most—90 percent—of the time and effort is spent in advance. Really thinking about who your audience will be is like washing and priming the surfaces, applying painter's tape, and putting down drop cloths. Preparing thoroughly before you apply paint takes time, but it clearly defines the surfaces to be painted, helps make sure the paint will stick, and prevents messes. Preparing thoroughly before you speak helps you be clear about both the scope and content of your information, helps you present information in a way that is likely to be understood and remembered, and prevents misunderstandings. Especially if presentations are new for you, you should plan to follow this guideline because it helps tremendously with the next steps.

I run on the road long before I dance under the lights.

MUHAMMED ALI

Once the prep work is done, you will be ready to create and organize the information that will become your notes. The ability to organize your content well and create useful notes is absolutely vital. The next chapter will help you learn to do this.

The methods you will learn will work in the real world. In an ideal world, you would have lots of time to prepare, but this is not an ideal world. In this world, the best-laid schemes of mice and men often go askew. Sometimes you need to prepare really, really fast! So Chapter 4 will help you quickly and easily prepare great notes.

Summary

When you can clearly state your presentation goals, you have taken the first important step toward achieving them. The next step is to gain an understanding of the needs and goals of your audience. Understanding the audience is vital so you can gather the right information, organize it appropriately, and deliver it in the most effective way. Three important considerations are the credibility you have with your audience, their psychographics, and their demographics.

To explore the needs and goals of your audience, you can survey individuals who will attend. Do this before your presentation in person, by phone, or with a prepared survey. You can also visit related Web sites and review literature such as corporate reports, product or service brochures, and industry publications.

Think about how to best tailor the information for a highly diverse audience. Develop a plan for presenting information to a diverse audience, and share your plan with them. Consider the language choices you make, the examples you use or stories you tell, your use of humor, and how you plan to encourage and answer questions from the audience.

4

GET IT TOGETHER

Construct First-Class Content

Preparing the Content

The amount of preparation to be done depends on a number of factors: the breadth and depth of your knowledge, the formality of the occasion, the audience, the length of the talk. It depends on whether you are most capable and comfortable with highly structured and detailed notes, or speaking more spontaneously.

Levels of Preparation

Three basic levels of preparation of content are none, some, and all.

- *Impromptu* means given with no notice—"off the cuff"—and without notes.

- *Extemporaneous* means delivered from notes or an outline but not memorized.

- *Memorized* and *scripted* mean every word is chosen in advance. Memorized talks may be delivered without notes, while scripted talks are generally read aloud.

While some situations may call for impromptu, memorized, or scripted presentations, most presentations today are extemporaneous. An extemporaneous presentation allows you to combine the benefits of preparation with those of a more natural, conversational, and flexible delivery. To use words borrowed from both Beerbohm and Hugo above, it gives us the benefits of improvisation without the fear of falling into a void. Using speaker notes is an important part of delivering information extemporaneously. Here are a few good reasons for choosing to speak extemporaneously, using notes that are separate from your slides. While you prepared and organized your notes, you will have thought through your information thoroughly. This makes you feel more confident.

Off-the-cuff presentations don't give you the opportunity to be as clear, well organized, or thorough as you can be with some preparation.

Second, putting all (or even most) of the things you want to say into slides almost always results in awful slides. They will take too much time to create, they will be too wordy, and there will be too many of them.

Third, reading word for word will sound stilted. You will not have good eye contact with your audience, so you will not look as confident or honest. You won't be able to observe your listeners' reactions and will miss opportunities to respond to puzzled expressions or dive more deeply into something that catches the listeners' attention.

> It isn't working that's so hard;
> it's getting ready to work.
>
> ANDY ROONEY

Fourth, memorizing a script and reciting it from memory will cause many of the same problems as reading the script. Since memory is unreliable under stress, you will be vulnerable to memory loss. Finally, unless memorizing is absolutely your only option, it is a terrible use of your time.

Getting Started

The rule-of-thumb advice for a presentation is to do three things:

1. Tell them what you're going to tell them.

2. Tell them.

3. Tell them what you told them.

This is good advice, but not specific enough to be very helpful. It does clearly recommend that you use a three-part presentation structure: an opening, a body, and a close. But how to actually develop and organize these three parts can still be a puzzle. So, specific directions on how to develop each of these three parts of your presentation follow. The approaches here will follow that classic rule above but also give you the instructions you need to do a great job with all three parts.

Develop Your Notes

The step-by-step process that follows is a simple one. You will learn two variations of the process and then choose the one that works best for you. With this process, you will be able to organize your content quickly. Next you can "tweak" your basic content to meet the need for more or less detail. You will then have notes that will let you abandon any fear of forgetting something important. You will have a strong opening and closing. You will have a clear structure, one that you have consciously chosen to help the audience follow your argument. Finally, you will have the flexibility of changing the order of points you cover as you speak and still get back on track.

Begin with the Middle in Mind

Let's start with the body of the presentation. Here's why. Once you have completed developing and organizing the body, you will be able to look at the "big picture" very clearly. Then you can make a fully informed decision about what to say in the opening and closing. The content of the opening and closing—both what to say and how to say it—should enhance the more fully developed information in the body. Like the front and back covers of a book, the opening and closing should complement contents within.

The Step-by-Step Process

Follow these four steps as you develop the body of your presentation:

1. Gather information.

2. Group it.

3. Structure it.

4. Edit it ruthlessly.

The first two steps—gather information and group it—can be interchanged if the situation calls for it, creating simple variations on the process. The variation to choose depends on how completely you mastered the content before you begin to organize it. The two variations of the step-by-step process are the "group and gather" approach and the "gather and group" approach.

The Gather and Group Approach

If you need to research, get input from others, and if your presentation will be creative or interpretive, this approach may be most useful.

Gather

First, gather information. As soon as your presentation is scheduled, designate a folder—paper or electronic—for notes. All your information now has a home. As you research, learn more, think of more you want to say, or remember questions you will need answered, make a note and put it in the folder. When you decide to organize and finalize your content you will already have a good start.

Before you begin to organize this information, add the information in your head to the information in your folder. Capture as many ideas or thoughts as you can, each on a separate note card or adhesive note. Add them to the information already in your folder. This process is often more fruitful if you do it in two or three sittings. Leaving and returning later can give you a fresh perspective and generate more and different information.

Group

When you have the needed information, group your information cards or adhesive notes by common or related ideas. Just scan your notes and get started. Our brains are hard-wired to categorize and group information. Your notes will almost arrange themselves into groups. Name each group, writing the name on a separate note: The names of the groups become your main points.

Legend has it that Abraham Lincoln used this method. According to the story, when engaged in the famous series of seven debates with Stephen A. Douglas in the summer and fall of 1858, Lincoln took notes as Douglas spoke, "filed" them in his stovepipe hat, and then spread them out on the floor at night to organize his responses and counterarguments. True or not, the story speaks to the power and simplicity of this approach.

The Group and Gather Approach

Use the group and gather approach when you have a very clear idea of the main points you want to make.

Group

Group first. Start with the main points you want to cover. A good way to do this is to jot each of these main points down on a separate sheet of paper. For example, if you are doing a project update presentation, your main points—and your page headings—may be:

1. Briefly review project goals, plan, and timeline

2. Review progress to date

3. Explain reasons for changes from timeline

4. Summarize how changes are being handled

5. Review revised timeline to completion

6. Handle questions

Gather

Then gather. Once you have identified and written down your main points, you are ready to gather and add information to support each one. Revisit each main point, each sheet of paper. Develop supporting information for one main point at a time. Jot down each supporting fact, point, or idea on a small adhesive note. Keep it with the main point—on the same page, literally. Allow yourself some flexibility. It is normal for your mind to flood with ideas and information once you get going. Don't edit now. The important point is to capture information as it occurs to you, even if it seems tangential to your main point or related to a different one. Capture as much information as possible in writing.

When you have supporting information for each of your main points, stop. Check each piece of supporting information for any tangential information you have created. Does it really belong under one of your main points? Is it on the right page? If not, move it. If it seems unrelated, put that note off to the side until later.

Now you can organize your main points into a logical and effective order. The best and most logical structure may be obvious. In the project update presentation outlined above, the logical structure is quite obvious. At times, the best structure may be less obvious. If so, consider the structures that follow.

Choose a Content Structure

Content can be organized in many ways, but you should be clear as to what that structure is. A clear structure prevents you from rambling and helps you remember what to say and when to say it. Your listeners should be able to identify that structure exists. This helps them follow and see both details and the bigger picture.

Choices of Structure

Most well-structured presentations fall into one of the following categories.

General to Specific

Start with a general overview or the establishment of a general concept. Then cover specifics pertinent to the particular audience. For example, say that your state is experiencing a budget crisis. State public school funding will be reduced next year. In your district, state funding will be cut by 12 percent. Then present ideas for raising money locally to help cover the cost of special education programs within your district.

Specific to General

This structure takes you from the components or details to the overall picture or result. For example, you report the major initiatives, successes, and earnings of each division of your corporation for the last year. Then you report overall corporate earnings.

Order of Importance

This structure has two forms. Presenting the most important information first satisfies those listeners who want you to "cut to the chase" but may sacrifice the building of suspense that will help keep the listeners' attention. Building to the most important information may create a sense of anticipation and excitement, but may frustrate those who want you to "cut to the chase." Will they still be listening when you get to the critical information? Choose based on your knowledge of your audience and purpose.

Order of Urgency

The order-of-urgency structure can also be used in two ways. You may start with the most urgent information, and move to the least urgent. The second is to start with the least urgent and move to the most urgent. These options have the advantages and disadvantages of the order of importance. Also, consider the implications of stating the most important action first. Will your audience remember it at the end? To make sure they do, restate it in your close.

Temporal

This structure follows a timeline or outlines a sequence of events. It avoids judgments about importance or urgency. It is useful for giving historical overviews and outlining the steps to follow in a schedule of events. For example, the history of United States naval uniforms in the early twentieth century might start with uniforms worn during the Philippine-American War (1899–1902), then move on to those of the Boxer Rebellion (1901–1902), the Latin American Campaigns (1906–1933), World War I (1917–1918), and the Yangtze Service (1926–1927 and 1930–1932). The temporal structure is often a component of the next two structures.

Geographic

The geographic structure follows the geography covered. A presentation on opportunities to market your products in the Pacific Rim might include a brief tour of the area. Moving clockwise, it might start with the North Pacific regions of Asia and eastern Russia; move to the Pacific regions of North America, Central America, and South America, then the Pacific Islands, New Zealand, Australia, and southern Asia; and end with Southeast Asia.

Cause and Effect

The cause-and-effect structure lists or explains the cause or causes of something, then presents the effect. For example, some of the heat-insulating tiles broke off the space shuttle *Columbia* during its launch. Reentry into the earth's atmosphere created intense heat. The missing tiles left the shuttle vulnerable to the heat. The vulnerability to heat resulted in structural failure. The shuttle broke up shortly before landing.

Procedure or Process

The procedure-or-process structure lists and explains a logical sequence of steps. Often, it explains the need for completing the steps in that order. For example, if you want an aquarium, start by researching aquariums to determine the best kind for you. Should you choose saltwater or fresh? How large? How much maintenance are you willing to do? How much do you want to spend? Next, purchase the aquarium and accessories. Set up the aquarium. Fill it with water. Add the necessary chemicals to balance the aquatic environment. Now it is safe to add fish.

Compare and Contrast

The compare-and-contrast structure compares two or more concepts or objects in one or more ways. For example, several products might be compared on the factors of quality, durability, ease of use, and price, to help determine the lowest total cost of ownership. Wines could be compared on the basis of sweetness versus dryness, sugar-to-acid balance, color, aroma, and the potential for aging well.

Pros and Cons

The pros-and-cons structure is similar to compare and contrast but also may examine just one concept or object or compare a proposed change to the status quo. It usually includes value judgments. A company considering whether to move its factory to another state may identify lower taxes and the local availability of raw materials as pros but the anticipated worker turnover, training, and relocation costs as cons.

Three Special Step-by-Step Structures

Special situations call for a special structure to both communicate clearly and manage the emotional response. These three have proven to do both well.

Sell a Product or Service

These five steps are good ones to use for a sales presentation.

1. First, show the need. Discuss why and how the listeners need what you have to offer. Acknowledge their situations, challenges, and goals. What problems occur that could be solved or prevented? What opportunities are lost without your offering? Can you give the listeners a bigger picture or a deeper understanding of their own needs? For example, will their current needs be intensified or changed by developing trends or anticipated changes in their environment?

2. Second, increase interest and emotion. What if the problems become more serious? If the need is real and urgent, meeting it will be interesting to the listeners. If the need is irritating, painful, or frightening, the solution will be met with enthusiasm, relief, gratitude, and probably other emotions as well. Remember that evoking emotion is a key to creating a long-term memory. Don't be too concerned with remaining logical and professional at this point. A little drama is a vital ingredient here.

3. Third, show how the product or service satisfies the need. Explain why having your product or service is the best way to satisfy the need. How is the product or service better—more functional, more reliable, more powerful, more effective, a better value—than any other solution? Testimonials, examples, demonstrations, and visual aids will all help you accomplish this step.

4. Fourth, help the audience members visualize using and benefiting from the product or service. Psychology of persuasion teaches us that belief follows action. When a person acts, that person will most likely find a way to believe that action is a good one, a logical one, and the best choice. By helping listeners imagine using and benefiting from what you offer, you help them persuade themselves. Paint a picture to help them imagine themselves working more easily, more efficiently, more reliably, and less expensively. How will they use the time, energy, or money they will save? Will they get credit for solving the problem? Will they be rewarded? How will they feel?

5. Fifth, request action or approval. Remember to close. Don't be shy. Define the next step you want your listeners to take. Ask directly for what you want. Then pause and wait for an answer.

Every presentation should be completed within the allotted period of time. This is especially true for sales presentations. Finishing early allows time for questions and discussions, and extensions to the allotted time should be at the request of the customer. Taking more than the allotted amount of time for the initial presentation is disrespectful and will annoy and alienate buyers. So time your presentation and tailor it accordingly.

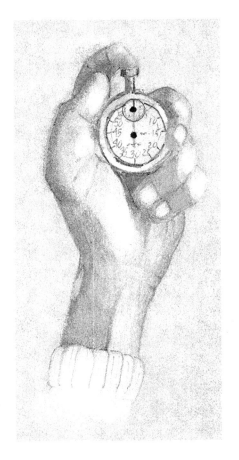

Report Bad News

These five steps will help you deliver bad news as effectively as possible. Here you sandwich the bad news between two positives.

1. Buffer the bad news with a positive or neutral statement. This helps prepare the audience for the bad news. Be honest and realistic. Use a positive tone and demeanor, but don't be overly optimistic or saccharine.

2. Connect to the bad news with a clear transition. Avoid making negative value judgments here. The listeners will come to their own conclusions when they hear the news.

3. Deliver the bad news. State it clearly. Do not hedge or try to soften it with obscure language. Report the facts you know. Explain why they happened or why they will happen. If more facts will come out later, state this.

4. Suggest alternatives. Alternatives soften the blow and help restore a sense of control. If these alternatives may change as new information comes in, tell your listeners this.

As you travel down life's highway…whatever be your goal, you cannot sell a doughnut without acknowledging the hole.

HAROLD J. SHAYLER

5. Rebuild goodwill. You may reinforce the positive, answer questions, listen to other suggestions, and so on.

Problem to Solution

These six steps are good basics to follow when discussing a problem and solution.

1. Define and limit the problem. A clear definition of the problem includes a statement of where the problem begins and ends.

2. List all the criteria the solution must meet. Listing the criteria helps you avoid wasting time and effort on solutions that aren't possible or practical to implement.

3. Identify possible solutions. Briefly state each one. Consider the order in which you introduce the possible solutions. It may make sense to order them from best to worst or worst to best.

4. Evaluate each solution against the criteria. When you evaluate the solutions, you might use one of the previous structures. For example, the pros-and-cons structure might be useful here.

5. Choose the best solution. Because you laid the groundwork to choose the solution that is most effective and practical, your choice is likely to be accepted and supported by your listeners.

6. Explain how the solution will be implemented. Include specifics. For example, list the steps to be taken. If possible, include individual responsibilities and the anticipated date of completion of each step.

Variations on this structure may be best for different problem situations. Consider the following questions as you decide whether a variation of the problem-solving structure is needed.

*   *How much do the listeners already know about the problem?* If they know little or nothing about the problem, more information about the problem itself may be needed. Consider using the cause-and-effect structure to explain the problem. If listeners are already very familiar with the problem, spend more time on the recommended

solutions. The six-step problem-solving structure may be a good one to use, with emphasis on steps 3, 4, and 5.

- *Has a solution already been implemented, or do you want to persuade your listeners to support the solution you recommend?* If one solution has already solved the problem, listeners may need less information about why it was chosen. If you must persuade the listeners to support a recommended solution, the six-step problem-solving structure may serve you well. This structure is a good one for outlining and explaining how you chose the solution you recommend. You may or may not choose to include step 6, discussing how the solution was, or will be, implemented.

Use Your Own Good Judgment to Choose a Structure

Your knowledge of your audience, your purpose, and your content will help you choose the best structure. It is possible that your presentation will not use one of the structures already discussed. You might find it appropriate to combine more than one of the suggested structures or modify one to better meet your needs. But before you finish your preparations, you should have a recognizable structure. Without it your presentation will not be as coherent or effective.

Presenting Information Within a Structure

Once you have organized your main and supporting points into a clear and logical structure, you can develop each of the points and ideas. How much detail does the audience need? How much do they want? How much can they handle?

The list below gives you a number of ways you can present information within the main structure of your presentation. You may have additional ideas that will work well.

Deliver what you promise the audience. That is, don't tell them you are going to outline if you plan to expound. Don't tell them that you will prove a point if you are actually going to interpret.

When you present information within a structure, you can:

- Analyze: Separate into essential parts and examine or interpret each part.

- Compare: Examine two or more things to identify similarities and differences.

- Conclude: End or close, including a summary, result, inference, or decision.

- Contrast: Set in opposition in order to show differences.

- Criticize: Judge merits and faults. Criticism often accompanies analysis.

- Define: State meaning of, explain qualities or nature of, determine limits of.

- Describe: Convey an image or impression with words that reveals the appearance or nature of; give an account of; list parts, qualities, and characteristics of.

- Discuss: Examine by argument, consider and debate the pros and cons of an issue, explain conflicts. Discussion often includes analysis, criticism, and comparison.

- Enumerate: Separately list several ideas, aspects, events, qualities, reasons.

- Evaluate: Appraise, determine value or amount of. Include evidence.

- Explain: Help understand, make clear the reason, assign meaning, interpret.

- Expound: Give a methodical, detailed, scholarly explanation.

- Illustrate: Explain using examples or comparisons.

- Interpret: Explain, construe, or understand in a certain way. Give the meaning of something by paraphrase.

- Outline: Give a general account or report limited to main points or features.

- Prove: Establish the truth or genuineness of by evidence or argument.

- Rate: Estimate quality or value, assign to a class, or assign comparative worth.

- Summarize: Briefly and concisely state or restate main points. Avoid unnecessary details. Include conclusions.

- Trace: Follow the course, development, or history of. Show the order of events or progress of a subject or event.

When the body of your presentation is done, you are ready to develop an opening and closing that will do it, you, and your audience justice.

Opening Your Presentation

Your opening should increase interest and emotion. Your goal is to earn the attention you are given—quickly. You need to leverage the power of the check-you-out moments.

The Check-You-Out Response

When you begin speaking, you will almost always have the attention of the audience. I call this initial attention the "check-you-out response." As you take your place and begin to speak, curiosity makes people look at and listen to you. You are the salient object—the center of attention. Audience members are curious, eager for the action to begin, hungry for information. You will not need to take extraordinary measures to grab attention.

But don't assume you will keep the audience's attention by continuing to speak. People need a reason to continue to pay attention. Sitting quietly is not the same as listening attentively. You must quickly convince them that paying attention is a good use of their time, that listening has value. You need to increase interest and tap into emotions to hold their attention beyond the check-you-out response.

You Compete for Attention During Your Presentation

As you speak, your competition becomes distractions, physical discomforts, and what is going on inside listeners' own heads. The most reliable way to earn their attention and keep it is to give them what they want.

Your Opening Should Answer Five Questions

Audience members want and need the answers to these five questions. A good opening provides the answers clearly and succinctly. Your job is to provide them.

1. What is this about? People are unlikely to come to a presentation without some knowledge of the topic and purpose. You can certainly confirm the subject of the presentation—the issue, the situation, the need, the problem, the opportunity—but your job will likely be to define and limit the topic more than actually introduce it. State the scope of your talk and the level of detail you will cover.

2. What do you believe? What do you believe about the subject? Why does it matter? How important is it? How urgent? Listeners want to know where the speaker really stands.

3. Why should I care? Why should the listeners care? What is at stake? What implications could it have? How could these affect the listeners? Why does it matter to them?

4. What do you want me to do? Here you have a great chance to move the listeners from a passive to active mode. Give them responsibility. Make them active intellectual and emotional partners in your talk. What do you want the listeners to do during your presentation? What do you want them to believe and do after listening? What action should they take? What specific types of approval and support should they give? How much? When do you need it?

5. Why should I? Why should listeners do this? How will the action you call for benefit the listeners? What needs of theirs will it satisfy? What will their reward be?

These questions should be answered as soon, as clearly, and as succinctly as possible. The majority of your opening remarks should consist of the answers to these five questions. Here is an example.

> "Good afternoon. Reducing the time it takes you to get a new product to market is critical to your continued success. I believe CX-FAB is a terrific tool because it will reduce the time it takes to develop and test a new product by an average of 30 percent. Please watch and listen as I explain the way you can achieve this speed by using CX-FAB. Feel free to stop me at any point to ask questions. As you listen, compare the process I describe to your current process, and learn how CX-FAB will simplify your design and test processes and reduce your time to market. Being first to market will give you the advantages of more market share, more profit, and continued leadership in the industry."

Let's look at how the five basic questions were answered to compose the core message.

1. *What is this about?* Getting new products to market quickly.

2. *What does the speaker believe?* CX-FAB is a terrific tool.

3. *Why should the listeners care?* Their success depends upon getting new products to market quickly.

4. *What should the listeners do?* They should listen and ask questions to learn and understand how CX-FAB works. They should compare how the CX-FAB works to the tools they use now.

5. *Why should they do this?* It will simplify the design and test processes, reduce the time to market, increase their market share and profit, and help them hold on to their leadership position in the industry.

Your Opening Is Almost Done

When you have answered these five questions clearly and succinctly, you have a robust opening. Other elements you may want to include in your opening follow. When you decide to include any of these elements, be brief. Remember that "less is more" as you put together your opening—the best way you can keep the attention of the audience is to get to the important information quickly.

Introductions

Will another person introduce you? Will you introduce yourself? Decide far enough in advance to avoid confusion or awkwardness. Then prepare accordingly.

Having someone else introduce you is often a good choice. It can be difficult to introduce one's self. We are socialized not to talk too freely about our accomplishments. We may be unsure of what to say or how much to include. Listing your accomplishments may help establish your credibility with the audience, but it can make you so uncomfortable that you minimize them or come across as nervous. On the other hand, it is easy for someone else to praise you and your accomplishments. This person can do so with respect, warmth, and a sense of pride in what you can offer the audience. If someone else will introduce you, make sure they have the appropriate information. This will help get you off to a strong start.

If you will introduce yourself, plan what to say. Be brief, but be sure to mention information that will establish your credibility. Include something that will help you connect emotionally with the audience—a bit about a personal experience or shared interest will often do the trick. A very brief introduction may be appropriate if you were first introduced some time ago, for example, if you are one of a series of speakers introduced at the beginning of the event. But avoid being too repetitious. This doesn't work well: "As it says on this first slide and on the program, and as Dr. Livingston just said when she introduced me, my name is Endless Lee Repeated." Instead, start with an important point.

If you will introduce and/or thank hosts, dignitaries, or colleagues, be prepared. Check for the correct names, titles, and pronunciations. Ask about any protocol issues, such as the proper rank order for the introductions.

"Thank You for Coming"

If you thank the audience for coming, it should sound genuinely felt. Use vocal tones that sound like you mean it. Avoid tired phrases like "I want to thank you for taking time out of your busy schedules" (to listen to you thank them for taking time out of their busy schedules?). Use a more original or personalized way to thank them. For example, you could mention what is making them so busy that their attendance shows real interest or commitment. If you really want to show gratitude for the time and attention you are given, give your listeners as much valuable information as possible in the time you have. If you finish a bit early, they will likely be grateful for the gift of time.

Opening Advice

Consider these points when planning your opening. Doing so will help you be succinct and set an appropriate tone for your presentation.

- Avoid stating the obvious. "I am here today to talk to you about" is obvious: You are obviously there, it is obviously today, and you are obviously talking. Instead, find a fresher way of introducing your topic. If the listeners already know what the topic is (and they almost always do), tell them why you will speak on it. Explain why it matters to them. Another good option is to limit the scope of your talk, that is, to state which parts of a larger issue or topic you will cover.

- For a talk on a specialized subject, state what level of knowledge you assume the listeners have. This is helpful and appreciated by mixed audiences. Mention how you will handle the differences.

- Welcome listeners only if you are the first speaker. If previous speakers have welcomed them, they will probably be grateful if you get right down to business.

- Don't apologize for your presence, your level of knowledge, or your state of readiness. Apologizing indicates lack of confidence and detracts from your credibility: "I know you were expecting Dr. Gold. I'm sure you're disappointed. She had to handle a personal emergency, so I'm filling in. I just found out a couple of hours ago, so bear with me. I know many of you know more about this topic than I do."

- Don't express surprise at how many (or few) people came. Expressing surprise sounds as if you were unprepared or out of touch. Expressing satisfaction or pleasure at the attendance is fine. Then give any information or instructions for resulting changes in timing, seating, and so on in a matter-of-fact tone.

- Try not to be the one to cover logistical details, such as locations of phones and bathrooms. If such details are needed, have someone cover them before you start. If you must, keep it brief. Pause for at least several seconds before beginning your actual presentation.

- At a venue with multiple speakers in multiple rooms, do a brief and clear "destination check." Wait until anyone who gets up to leave is out of the room (or at least out of the main body of the audience and into an aisle). A destination check might sound like this: "This is the presentation on genetic modification of native perennial crops. The presentation on cloning with short telomeres is in the Cypress Ballroom." (Pause)

Before you decide to include the elements just covered, decide if you really need them. Covering the whole list could take a great deal of time. They may be unnecessary, may be done by others, or could be done one-on-one outside the context of the presentation. Find out early and plan accordingly.

Opening a Presentation to a Reluctant Audience

While most audiences are predisposed to give you their attention as you begin, you may occasionally face a situation when this is not true. If listeners are "drafted" to attend, if you are one of a series of speakers, if the room is very warm or dark, if some listeners are feeling the effects of jet lag or a cocktail party last night, you face more of a challenge.

If you do something to compensate for such things, do something that isn't shopworn. Many ways of opening a presentation have long lost their ability to engage the audience. They no longer contain any elements of surprise or novelty. I would be happy if I never again heard a speaker begin by reading the dictionary definition of the topic!

Good ways to earn the attention of the audience are the same techniques that create a feeling of dialogue with the audience. These are covered in more depth in Chapter 10, but here are some to consider.

- Ask a rhetorical question. Then pause to let the audience members think.

- Ask a question and request a show-of-hands response.

- Deliver late-breaking news.

- Share a startling fact or statistic.

- Tell a brief story or relate an anecdote.

- Use a powerful visual aid.

- Share a thought-provoking quotation.

Opening a Presentation to a Hostile Audience

Three steps can help you get off to a successful start when you are faced with the challenge of presenting to a hostile audience.

1. Thank the audience sincerely. A simple but sincere thank-you for coming helps establish a cooperative and respectful tone. Avoid the temptation to preach: "I'm sure we all appreciate the importance of having a complete understanding of this issue. Be open-minded."

2. Establish common ground. Briefly stress what you can agree on, for example, "We all have very strong feelings about this issue" or "We all want as much information as we can get. We need to learn everything we can to make sure nothing like this ever happens again."

3. Use the appropriate nonverbal delivery skills. Stay conscious of the unspoken signals you give. Now is not the time to seem arrogant, condescending, or aloof. Review the information on nonverbal communication in Chapter 8. Avoid defensive or aggressive behavior.

Close Your Presentation

Few words perk up an audience like the words "lastly," "finally," and "in conclusion." Use the attention you have to your advantage. Closing is your opportunity to pull concepts together, reinforce information, motivate the listeners to action, and leave your listeners thinking about how they can benefit from what you recommend.

As you develop your close, think about that old advice: Tell them what you are going to tell them; tell them; tell them what you told them.

Assuming you did tell them, in more detail, what you promised in the opening, and that your presentation made it clear why they should care, your closing should sound a lot like your opening. Let's revisit the list of questions you answered as you opened your presentation. Again, an opening should answer:

- What is this about?

- What do you believe?

- Why should the listeners care?

- What do you want them to do?

- Why should they?

Assuming there is now no need to state what a just completed presentation was about, let's look more closely at the other three questions.

1. *What do you believe?* Speaking with the credibility you have just earned, your belief is more compelling and persuasive than it was when you opened. Here are examples of leveraging that credibility in a belief statement.

   - "Now you can understand fully why I believe that this project will be a terrific investment."

   - "Each factor I discussed shows why I have complete faith in our ability to beat the deadline."

   - "So all the evidence, statistical and anecdotal, leads me to think that the shift is not just likely, but inevitable."

2. *What do you want me to do?* The call to action is often the most important part of your presentation. Now your audience is as likely as they ever will be to take the action you recommend. Your information is fresh in their minds, they are sitting with other like-minded people, and your credibility is at its highest. Here are examples of a call to action.

- "Starting immediately, use these criteria every time you make a decision on a commercial loan."

- "Have your selections on my desk by the first of December."

- "Stop by our booth this afternoon to see a demonstration, and let us know when you would like an on-site demo."

- "Will you approve this project today?"

3. *Why should I?* People will act in self-interest. Remind them of the benefits that will follow if they take the action you recommend. Here are some examples of benefit statements.

- "This reduced loan losses 15 percent in the New York market. It will give us the profitability we need to move into new markets. That means new opportunities—and bigger bonuses."

- "We'll design based on your individual needs and preferences. You'll pay for just the features you need."

- "Less downtime, access to information instantly, and now you can really do target marketing. This changes the game!"

- "Your approval means we can start next week and finish construction in time to move in October. And the costs can go on the books for this year."

I have been a selfish being all my life, in practice, though not in principle.
JANE AUSTEN

The following example is a close from a TED talk about the leak of the Panama Papers by Robert Palmer, Banks and Corruption Campaign Leader for Global Witness. Palmer clearly and succinctly answers these three questions.

What do you believe?

"One of the things that is sad is that, actually, the US is lagging behind. There's bipartisan legislation that had been introduced in the House and the Senate, but it isn't making as much progress as we'd like to see. So we'd really want to see the Panama leaks, this huge peek into the offshore world, be used as a way of opening up in the US and around the world. For us at Global Witness, this is a moment for change."

What do you want me to do?

"We need ordinary people to get angry at the way in which people can hide their identity behind secret companies. We need business leaders to stand up and say, 'Secrecy like this is not good for business.' We need political leaders to recognize the problem, and to commit to changing the law to open up this sort of secrecy."

Why should I?

"Together, we can end the secrecy that is currently allowing tax evasion, corruption, money laundering to flourish."[20]

Include Other Information If Needed

Optional elements you may choose to include in your closing follow. But remember: A succinct closing will be more powerful than one that is drawn out.

- Summarize the main points.

- Make recommendations.

- Ask a rhetorical question to leave the audience thinking.

- Use a quotation to reinforce your message.

- Ask for comments.

- Ask for questions.

- Thank the audience or hosts.

If You Want an Outline

Now you can use the information you have on your cards or adhesive notes to assemble an outline. Use only the words you need to remind you of the points you want to make. Try to avoid writing complete sentences; you will do a better job of speaking conversationally and naturally if you don't stick to a script. Rather, practice looking at the points and putting the ideas into words as if you were talking comfortably with a small group of people

Edit Ruthlessly

Time it. Talk through your presentation out loud. It likely takes longer than you think. The details of the information you now have will almost always be more precious to you than they are to your audience. Most business presentations would only be improved by ruthless editing. Follow these tips to shorten, tighten, and sharpen the messages in your talk.

- Limit the information about you and your organization. Cover what will help you achieve the credibility and rapport you need, but then get to the information your listeners need.

- Cut the information about how you prepared for the presentation. This is your past business. The business of the audience now is to hear what you have to say. If you are a consultant and feel a need to justify your fee, limit the explanation of your approach and research. Can you briefly explain what the audience needs to know about your research methods before you report each finding or make a recommendation?

- Shorten your sentences. Long, complex sentences often have to be explained or clarified with other long, complex sentences.

- Limit adverbs and adjectives. Use nouns and verbs. Eliminate any adverbs and adjectives that aren't necessary. Be ruthless in deciding what qualifies as "necessary."

- Eliminate redundancies and information that is not germane. Redundancies can occur in phrasing: "We need a qualified expert to identify the basic fundamentals and identify different alternatives that will lead to a new breakthrough." Examples, analogies, anecdotes, stories that illustrate, explain, prove, or bring information to life are germane—they increase understanding and impact. Too many become meaningless.

- Cut slick transitions. Slick is not genuine. If your presentation flows too smoothly, it can lull your listeners to sleep. Use transitions to link ideas when necessary. Use a pause as the "white space" to separate sections or emphasize a point.

- Cut tentative language. Tentative language makes you sound less confident and reduces the perceived importance of your information: "Hopefully you will perhaps consider thinking about this little proposal sometime when you find you have the time in the not-so-distant future." Not likely.

- Record yourself. Listen for "static." Do you hear "ah," "um," "you know," or "okay" repeatedly? Do you say "actually," "basically," or "simply" when you don't need to? Pause instead.

Time yourself again. Repeat as needed.

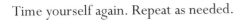

Summary

How you prepare and organize your content will depend on many factors. But some preparation is essential. Use the list below to be sure you have done the essentials in organizing your content.

Make sure your opening earns attention and gives the audience a reason to listen to more. The closing should include a call to action and a benefit to the audience for taking that action.

The structure should support the nature of your content. It should make it easy to follow your thought process or argument. Longer and more complex presentations benefit from clear transitions between sections.

Consider how much detail your listeners need, want, can handle, and can remember. Then decide how you should best present your information and develop your arguments. Keep in mind the time you have, and allow a little extra for unexpected changes in plan.

Find out who will do introductions. What will be said? Do the right people have the right information? Who will cover logistical information, such as instructions to the audience on the schedule, facilities, refreshments, and any changes in plans?

Decide when and how you will handle questions from the audience, and communicate this clearly at the beginning of your talk. Remember, long presentations will often be more effective if they include intermittent question-and-answer sessions.

5

When there is a gap between one's real and
one's declared aims, one turns as it were
instinctively to long words and exhausted idioms,
like cuttlefish squirting out ink.

GEORGE ORWELL

WORDS THAT WORK

The What and Why of Word Choice

L isteners much prefer a genuine and natural speaker. The right words will help you sound sincere and conversational. Yet some speakers fall into the habit of using words that come across as pretentious or pompous. Consider the case of Brad Marshall.

Brad Marshall, Wednesday, 9:40 a.m., leaving a voice mail:

"John, hi. Brad Marshall at Company Bee. Here's the update. WA 2 GO sales came in way over plan—we beat the last revision! I want to get together ASAP to work on sourcing parts…"

Brad Marshall, Wednesday, 10 a.m., giving a presentation:

Those who run to long words
are mainly the unskillful
and tasteless; they confuse
pomposity with dignity,
flaccidity with ease, and bulk
with force.

W. FOWLER

"Good morning. Ah, thank you for taking the time out of your busy schedules to join me here today. We made a commitment to you last quarter to significantly increase sales of the WA 2 GO. I am pleased to report that we have exceeded our market objectives, and sales exceeded our specified objectives, even those determined and established as a result of the most recent reassessment. In fact, the objectives were also exceeded by a margin that is, ah, exceedingly gratifying.

"However, at the present time we believe it is incumbent upon us to investigate alternative and additional potential supply sources for key product components…"

What happened to Brad Marshall? Brad fell victim to the belief that listeners will be impressed if we use fancy language. This is not true.

The Long and Short of It

More words may not make an idea clearer. If a longer phrase has shades of meaning important to your goal, use it. If not, choose the clear and concise short form, as shown in Table 5.1.

Table 5.1 Long or Short

Long	Short
except in a small number of instances	usually
a great number of times	often/frequently
for a brief period of time	briefly
bring to a conclusion	end
direct your attention to	look at
contingent upon	depends on
at this location	here
at that location	there
because of the fact that	because
afford an opportunity	allow/permit
for the reason that	because
in conjunction with	with
in the absence of	without
in the event of	if
in the occurrence of	if it happens
it is often the case that	often
make a decision	decide
if that is/were in fact the case	if
in spite of the fact that	although
in the event that	if
at the present time	now
in the near future	soon
in the direction of	toward
due to the fact that	because
a small number of	few
a large number of	many
a percentage of	some
a high percentage of	most
in many instances	often
in the majority of instances	usually
subsequent to	after
prior to	before
submit an application	apply

Fancy or Strong

The simpler, stronger word (Table 5.2) is usually the better choice. Use the fancy word if it has a shade of meaning important for your message, but if you use it just to impress, it can sound stilted, affected, or pompous.

Table 5.2 Fancy or Strong

Fancy	Strong
abandon	end, leave
abolish	end, stop
beneficial	good, helpful
benign	harmless
characteristic	typical
cognizant	aware
collaborate	work together
commence	start
component	part
compensation	pay
conceal	hide
contingent upon	depends on
demonstrate	show
deviate	vary, change
disadvantageous	bad, harmful
discontinue	end
disingenuous	insincere
elucidate	explain
encounter	meet
endeavor	try
enumerate	list
envision	see
expedite	streamline
fabricate	make
fluctuate	change, vary
institute	start, begin
ingenuous	sincere
intelligent	smart
judicious	wise
materialize	appear
maximum	most
minimum	least
prior to	before
pursuant to	following
subsequent to	after
utilize	use

Redundancy

Redundancy is the use of more words or phrases than needed to get the job done. Redundancy can be used effectively to emphasize or reinforce, but when redundant phrases sneak in accidentally, they clutter and weaken a message.

Redundancy can occasionally be used to add shades of meaning. "Past history" is redundant because all history is in the past. But "recent history" and "ancient history" increase understanding with added specificity. "Complete opposite" and "diametric opposite," while redundant, can be used to emphasize the idea of a great difference.

Use redundancies sparingly and consciously. The phrases in the first column of Table 5.3 are redundancies. The second column shows a simpler, nonredundant choice.

Table 5.3 Redundant Phrases

Redundant	Nonredundant	Redundant	Nonredundant
advance forward	advance	mutual cooperation	cooperation
any and all	any, all	new breakthrough	breakthrough
approximate estimate	estimate	new innovation	innovation
ask the question	ask	one and the same	the same
assemble together	assemble	one particular case	one case
basic essentials	basics, essentials	one specific example	one example
basic fundamentals	basics, fundamentals	one specific reason	one reason
close proximity	close	only single	only, single
combine together	combine	part and parcel	part
completely finished	finished	partial section	section
complete opposite	opposite	past experience	experience
component parts	components, parts	past history	history
connect together	connect, join	period of time	period
consensus of opinion	consensus, agreement	personal friend	friend
continue to remain	remain	personal opinion	opinion
contributing factor	factor	plan ahead	plan
cooperate together	cooperate	plan for the future	plan
diametric opposite	opposite	plan in advance	plan
different alternative	alternative	postpone until later	postpone
each and every	each, every	qualified expert	expert
early in the beginning	early	reason why	reason
end result	result	recur again	recur
entirely finished	finished	refer back	refer
exactly identical	identical	repeat again	repeat
experienced expert	expert	retreat back	retreat
few in number	few	resulting effect	result, effect
final conclusion	conclusion	same exact	same
final ending	ending	same identical	same
follow after	follow	seems apparent	seems, is apparent
full to capacity	full	separate and distinct	separate, distinct
join together	join	small-sized	small
joint partnership	partnership	still remain	remain
large-sized	large	sudden surprise	sudden, surprise
last of all	last	throughout the entire	throughout
main essentials	essentials	true fact	fact
might possibly	might	unanswered question	question
mix together	mix	unsolved problem	problem
more preferable	preferable	very unique	unique

Clichés

A cliché is a phrase that was originally effective and vivid but has become trite or banal through overuse. Presentations with too many clichés will lose freshness, originality, and emotional punch. Clichés can sound manipulative, even dishonest, if used to try to bolster a weak argument or to excuse bad behavior. "Absence makes the heart grow fonder" is not a legitimate excuse for ignoring an important relationship. And "out of sight, out of mind" is not a good reason to pester another person mercilessly.

Sometimes a cliché can be turned on itself to support your meaning. Consider "bedfellows make strange politics" and Oscar Wilde's "Truth is never pure, and rarely simple." Sometimes a minor change creates a humorous allusion to a cliché. Fred Allen's "Imitation is the sincerest form of television" is an example of the amusing use of a minor change.

Use clichés sparingly, and use them when they fit your topic precisely. If the cliché draws attention to itself, it is probably not appropriate. Table 5.4 lists common clichés.

Table 5.4 Clichés to Avoid

a finger in every pie	acid test
a word to the wise	as high as a kite
armed to the teeth	at the end of the day
at his fingertips	bite the dust
bite the bullet	cover your butt
by word of mouth	cut to the quick
cut and dried	give the green light
follow in the footsteps of	head in the clouds
got a gut feeling	if it ain't broke, don't fix it
hard and fast	keep your fingers crossed
hold your horses	line of least resistance
keep our options open	long row to hoe
kill two birds with one stone	make tracks
lock, stock, and barrel	nip it in the bud
make a long story short	no news is good news
needless to say	not playing with a full deck
no good deed goes unpunished	nothing ventured, nothing gained
no pain, no gain	pack a punch
nothing to write home about	peel the onion one layer at a time
old as dirt	playing with fire
poetry in motion	pull strings
put it on the back burner	road test
separate the men from the boys	ships that pass in the night
signed, sealed, and delivered	small potatoes
stick to it like glue	stick your neck out
sweep it under the carpet	talking about apples and oranges
the tip of the iceberg	the whole kit and caboodle
there are two sides to every question	there's no fool like an old fool
touch and go	turn back the clock
upset the apple cart	when the cat's away the mice will play
you can't win them all	you can't teach an old dog new tricks

Clichés As Excuses

The business world is plagued by clichés. Jeff Haden, contributing editor of *Inc.*, identified ten of the worst. In *10 Stupid Phrases the Worst Bosses Love to Use*, Haden identifies ten clichés that have become platitudes. Haden advises, "Platitudes aren't just annoying. Resorting to platitudes shows you don't want to listen, don't want to take action…in short, don't want to buckle down and do your job." Here are some of the platitudes Haden says are the worst offenders:

1. "Work smarter, not harder."

2. "There is no I in team."

3. "Perception is reality."

4. "Failure is not an option."

5. "It is what it is."[21]

Active and Passive Voice

"I found that…" is an example of the active voice.

"It has been shown that…" is an example of the passive voice.

When using the passive voice, the speaker puts the object before the subject, as in *the box was lifted by the woman*, instead of the subject before the object, as in *the woman lifted the box*. You can often recognize the passive voice by the extra verb needed. In the example just given, the passive voice uses *was lifted* rather than the *lifted* used by the active voice.

Unless you have a clear reason for choosing to use the passive voice, use the active voice. The passive voice can lead to ambiguity, and first-person pronouns are more effective than awkward or ambivalent sentences.

Technical and scientific speakers tend to overuse the passive voice. With use of the scientific method and the rigor of experimental design, great value is placed on "letting the facts speak for themselves." Personal opinion is deemed less important than data, logic, and intellectual rigor. But many general or business listeners interpret the use of the passive voice as a lack of personal conviction or confidence. When you overuse the passive voice, you seem reluctant to speak with conviction, take a stand, or accept responsibility.

Table 5.5 Active and Passive Voice

Passive	Active
It is well known that	I know, we know
It has been reported that	Reports tell us
It is widely believed	Many of us believe
It may be worth considering	Let's consider
These rules are outlined in section 12	Section 12 outlines these rules
The changes were seen beginning in phase 3	The changes began in phase 3
Extra attention should be given to step one	Step one should get extra attention
A form should be filled out by all associates	All associates should fill out a form

Some general guidelines to help you decide when the active voice or the passive voice is your best choice are:

- Choose active by habit, passive by conscious choice.

- Do not use passive to avoid using first-person pronouns (I, we, us).

- Do use passive when the action is more important than the actor. For example, "an agreement is reached," or "a major change is announced."

- Do use passive when you want to avoid assigning blame. For example, "a deadline was missed," or "a ball was dropped."

Positive and Negative Voice

The positive voice communicates confidence and is more inspiring. Consider the difference between "I can't comment on that" and "I can tell you this…"

Use the negative voice when you want to emphasize gravity, risk, and danger. Consider the difference between "Wear a seat belt to stay safe" and "Without seat belts, tragedies are inevitable."

Jargon and Specialized Language

Every field, trade, and profession has its own jargon—words that are understood in the intended sense by those in that specialty. Within a group, jargon and specialized language streamline communication. When all members of the group understand them, they can build rapport and foster a feeling of solidarity.

As knowledge increases and more specialties emerge, jargon and specialized language increase accordingly. Collaboration between specialists in related fields—and between companies—means that the use of jargon and specialized language can cause communication failures.

Jargon and specialized language create challenges for the presenter. They confuse those who don't understand what it means, cause frustration, and divide your listeners. If you plan to use a specialized term that is new to your listeners, think about when and how you will define it.

Inclusive Language

Inclusive language is language that does not exclude people from being seen as part of a group. Inclusive language is free from words, phrases or tones that reflect prejudiced, stereotyped, or discriminatory views of particular people or groups. It avoids implicit assumptions about people regardless of age, ability/disability, appearance, ethnicity, gender expression and gender identity, level of education, marital status, race, religion, sexual orientation, or socioeconomic status.

Using inclusive language often depends on understanding ways that language can unconsciously make assumptions about people. Consider this statement by presidential candidate John Kasich:

> "And how did I get elected? We just got an army of people who, um, and many women, who left their kitchens to go out and go door to door and to put yard signs up for me."[22]

These guidelines clarify the principles used to achieve inclusive language.

- *Put the person before the situation or limitation.* Say, "a person diagnosed with autism," rather than "an autistic person." Use "employees with visual impairment" rather than "visually impaired employees."

- *Emphasize abilities rather than limitations.* Say, "He uses a prosthetic for walking and running," rather than "He can't walk without his prosthetic leg."

- *Avoid language that overextends or overemphasizes.* Say, "She lives with severe arthritis" rather than "She suffers from crippling arthritis."

- *Mention group affiliation only when relevant.* For example, avoid, "Thank you all, young and old, for coming to celebrate the opening of our new library," and say, "Thank you for coming to celebrate the opening of our new library."

- *Put the person or people before the affiliation.* "People of color" is a synonym for all non-white people and may also be used to describe groups such as "physicians of color" or "women of color." "Colored people" has come to be offensive, has historically referred only to Black folks, and should not be confused with the broader category of "people of color."

- *Ascribe the affiliation correctly.* "People of color" is not a synonym for all minorities. For example, a white man with a disability is not a person of color, but does belong to a minority group.

The English language tradition of using the term "man" to refer to a human being, regardless of gender, has been problematic. Growing awareness and understanding of the importance of using inclusive language means that, in common usage, many older, gender-specific terms have been replaced by more inclusive terms. Table 5.6 lists some gender-specific terms and accepted gender-inclusive terms.

Inclusive Pronouns

For many decades, the phrases "he or she," "him or her," or "she/he" were accepted as grammatically correct ways to refer to a specific individual whose gender is irrelevant or unknown in context. For example, "When an adventurous person has options, he or she may decide to flip a coin."

However, these phrases are increasingly seen as problematic because they reinforce the idea that absolutely all people fall into strictly binary gender identities. The alternative is to use the singular form of "they." For example, "When an adventurous person has options, they may decide to flip a coin." Using "they" in the singular form may have once made you seem uneducated or inarticulate, but it is now widely understood to be a necessary replacement for the phrase "he or she." In fact, singular "they" was voted 2015 word of the year by the American Dialect Society.[23] Many individuals who identify as non-binary ask that others refer to them using they/them pronouns. For example, "Jamie is the CFO. They have held that position for 5 years."

Another approach is to use plural forms, such as "people" instead of "person" or "clients" instead of "the client." Then, with the second reference, you can use the plural "they" to avoid a gender-specific pronoun.

As society and culture evolve, so does the use of inclusive language. If in doubt of the accepted terms, there are current online sources for speakers and writers available to help you make appropriate choices.

Table 5.6 Gender-Specific and Gender-Neutral Terms

Gender Specific	Gender Neutral
brotherhood	community, kinship
chairman	chairperson, chair
cleaning lady	cleaner, housekeeper
delivery man	deliverer, courier, messenger
fellowship	camaraderie, support
fireman	firefighter
fraternal	warm, close, intimate
gentleman's agreement	informal/honorable agreement
housewife, househusband	homemaker
ladylike	courteous, cultured
maiden name	birth name
mailman	mail carrier
man (verb)	staff, run
manhood	adulthood
man-hour	staff hour
man-made	manufactured, synthetic
master (adjective)	expert, accomplished
master (noun)	owner, expert
master (verb)	learn, accomplish, succeed
mastermind	creator, launcher, visionary
masterpiece	great work, work of genius
masterplan	vision, comprehensive plan
middleman	go-between, broker
mother tongue	native language
motherly	nurturing, loving, caring
ombudsman	troubleshooter
repairman	service technician
salesman, saleslady	salesperson
spokesman	spokesperson
statesman	diplomat, political leader
to a man	without exception
waiter, waitress	server
watchman	security guard
workman	worker
workmanship	quality of construction

Precision of Word Choice

Using the wrong word can be embarrassing. Having someone in your audience ask, "Did you really mean that, or did you mean this?" can be even more embarrassing. But if use of the wrong word is not questioned, your true meaning is never understood and listeners can miss your intended meaning.

The list that follows includes some of the words misused most often in business presentations. You can quiz yourself to check that you use them correctly.

> Precision of communication is important, more important than ever, in our era of hair-trigger balances, when a false or misunderstood word may create as much disaster as a sudden thoughtless act.
>
> JAMES THURBER

Administrate or Administer?

Administer is a verb. Administration is a noun. Administrate has become commonly used as a verb in recent years. Does usage determine accepted use? You decide. I recommend using administer.

Affect or Effect?

Affect is a verb with two different meanings. It means "to cause a change in," as in "She believes strongly that an appreciation of the fine arts can positively affect the lives of people of all ages." It also means "to pretend to have." For example, "He affected an interest in ballet until after their fourth date."

Effect is a verb and means "to make happen." For example, "When dishonesty is discovered it can effect consternation and disappointment." It is also a noun and means "a result." For example, "He believes that the effect of his behavior did irreparable damage to their relationship."

Aggravate or Irritate?

Aggravate means "to make worse."

Irritate means "to annoy, bother, make angry, to inflame."

Example: "Don't irritate your listeners by using the wrong word. It could aggravate an uncomfortable situation."

Allusion or Illusion?

Allusion means "an indirect, passing, or casual reference."

Illusion means "an unreal image" or "a false impression, a mistaken view of reality."

Example: "In the first stanza of the poem there was an allusion to Shakespeare's Sonnet 18. This gave the illusion that the writer was familiar with the message of the sonnet."

Alternate or Alternative?

Alternate means "every other one in a series." If the series is a series of only two, alternate may mean "substitute."

Alternative means "one of two possibilities" and connotes a matter of choice that is not present with alternates.

Example: "The current supplier delivers on alternate days. We recommend you use them as your primary source but have an alternative in case their ability to deliver is ever interrupted."

Anticipate or Expect?

Anticipate means "to foresee," "to look forward to," or "to act in advance so as to prevent."

Expect also means "to look forward to" but also "to believe to be probable, to presume." Use expect in the sense of simple expectation.

Example: "We expect to meet the deadline because we have addressed all the anticipated difficulties."

Anxious, Eager, or Enthusiastic?

Anxious means "a state of unease or worry."

Eager means "a state of enthusiastic desire or interest."

Enthusiastic means "an intense feeling for a subject or cause," "eagerness, zeal," or "something inspiring."

Anxious has a negative connotation. Eager and enthusiastic may at times be used interchangeably, but both have positive connotations.

Example: "They are anxious because the delay has not been explained, but are eager for it to arrive. And they are so enthusiastic about putting it to use!"

Compose, Comprise, or Constitute?

Compose means "to make up of parts." For example, "The medley was composed of a series of show tunes." When used this way, compose is used with the word "of." Compose also means "to make tranquil or calm." For example, "Compose yourself."

Comprise means "to include, to contain, to be made up of," as in "The winning choral group comprises singers of all ages." Comprise is used without the word "of."

Constitute can be used as a substitute for compose, meaning "to make up." It is most often used in the context of politics, as in "to enact, to designate for an office, to appoint."

Continual or Continuous?

Continual means "recurring regularly and frequently."

Continuous means "uninterrupted in time or sequence."

Example: "The continuous rapid flow of the river calls for continual ferry service."

Credible, Creditable, or Credulous?

Credible means "believable or trustworthy."

Creditable means "praiseworthy or honorable."

Credulous means "gullible" or "ready to believe on insufficient evidence."

Example: "In the presence of such credulous jurors, credible witnesses were not necessary for conviction. That conviction was not evidence of a creditable prosecutor."

Fewer or Less?

Fewer is the comparative form of few. It usually refers to things that are counted by units: "fewer barrels of oil."

Less is one of the comparative forms of little. It is used to refer to mass or bulk items, as in "less oil."

Imply or Infer?

Imply means "to express indirectly, to suggest or indicate."

Infer means "to conclude by reasoning" or "to deduce from evidence."

Example: "Love of poetry implies a thoughtful and artistic nature. We inferred from their knowledge of the lives of English poets that they had studied them in depth."

Lay or Lie?

Lay means "to place, put, or set." Lay and the other principal parts of this verb (past, laid; past participle, laid) must have an object. For example, "Please promise to lay them down as soon as they fall asleep," "When setting the table, lay the salad forks next to the dinner plates," and "We laid out as many details as possible under the changing circumstances."

Lie means "to rest or recline, to be in a horizontal or recumbent position, to assume such a position." Lie and the other principal parts of this verb (lay, lain) are used without an object. For example, "I plan to lie here for another hour. So, go away," "I lay on there for two hours," and "I could have lain there much longer if the fire alarm had not gone off."

Momentarily or Soon?

Momentarily means "lasting only a moment" or "from moment to moment." It is so often used to mean "soon" that this use is becoming accepted. But save a moment and yourself four syllables and use "soon."

Orient or Orientate?

Orient means "to determine the bearings of" or "to make or become familiar with a situation." It has become common to use oriented to mean placing value or emphasis, as in "They are result-oriented."

Orientate means "to orient." Why use orientate when the less pretentious orient means the same thing? But then, do you really need to use either? Can you find a simpler way to express the thought, such as "They want results" or "They get results"?

Preventive or Preventative?

Preventive is an adjective.

Preventative is an adjective or a noun.

Example: "Preventive maintenance is vital when you need to maximize uptime with complex systems, and regular preventive maintenance is the best preventative."

> Like knowing some French or making sure not to say "irregardless," having a BA is a class marker in America.
>
> JOHN MCWHORTER

Regardless or irregardless?

Regardless of what you might have heard, there is no such word as irregardless.

Summary

Your message can be missed or misunderstood if not delivered clearly. The right words are important.

Speak simply. Shorter and stronger words, phrases, and sentences are almost always best.

Avoid redundancy to both shorten and strengthen your message.

Use clichés sparingly and only when they fit your topic precisely.

Make a habit of using the active rather than the passive voice. Use the passive voice only by conscious choice, because it can create a sense of vagueness, evasiveness, ambivalence, or reluctance to accept responsibility.

Use the positive rather than the negative voice by habit. The positive voice communicates confidence and is more inspiring. Use the negative voice by conscious choice to emphasize gravity, risk, or danger.

Words that engage the five senses will engage your audience. Shorter, stronger verbs create a sense of urgency.

Use inclusive language to avoid the impression that you make false assumptions about gender, marital status, ethnicity, and age.

Use words, phrases, acronyms, and industry terms that listeners understand. If you must use a specialized term, define it, especially with diverse audiences.

Use the right word. Familiarize yourself with the differences in meaning between often used similar words.

6

I have a theory about the human mind.
A brain is a lot like a computer. It will only take so
many facts, and then it will go on overload and blow up.

ERMA BOMBECK

RISE ABOVE THE NOISE

Make It Meaningful and Memorable

Think back to last weekend. Do you remember your conversations—all those you spoke with and what exactly was said—from those hours? Now, try to remember any of the commercial messages you were exposed to during those hours? Do you remember any specific online ads, TV commercials, radio ads, billboards, and messages on food packaging or grooming products? Chances are you can remember very little. Without conscious thought our minds filter out most of the information our nervous system delivers.

The good news: This is normal and healthy.

The bad news: Your listeners will do the same with the information you deliver.

Filters Let Us Focus

We filter to focus on what really matters. Without filtering we would be overwhelmed by information and sensation. Background noises, side conversations, lights, colors, even the pressure of our own clothes on our skin would all be constant distractions. If we were able to ignore the truly mundane and retain only facts, statistics, and "intellectual material," our difficulties would not be over. People with superhuman memories, able to recall vast databases of facts and statistics, are often incapable of abstract thought. Without the ability to discriminate, to ignore some things and focus on what really matters, we could not make sense of the world around us

Just because you talk does not mean people will listen. Even if they listen and hear you, they may not fully understand what you said, how you meant it, and probably will not remember much of what you say.[24] Most of what you say will be briefly considered and then forgotten.

> All thought is a feat of association.
>
> ROBERT FROST

Knowing listeners filter information as you speak, how can you increase the chance that your information will make it past the filter to the conscious mind? What are the qualities of information that are not just briefly considered, but really "taken to heart"—committed to long-term memory for later use? Information committed to long-term memory usually has one—or better, both—of these two qualities:

Familiar Information

Our brains operate by making connections, by storing information in overlapping "sets" and "subsets." Think of information as the human race. Some of us are siblings, some members of the same nuclear families, some distant cousins, some friends, some colleagues, some brief acquaintances, and some complete strangers. The brain considers incoming information and places new information with the "relatives and friends" of that information, not with complete strangers. When someone says, "It's a lot like…" or "That reminds me of…" they demonstrate the mental tendency to seek similarities and connections.

> The more connections that can be made in the brain, the more integrated the experience is within memory.
>
> DON CAMPBELL

Emotional Information

Emotional information doesn't mean high drama. Humans look for opportunities to experience pleasure and avoid pain. We are "hardwired" to act to maximize our opportunities for reward and minimize the chances of discomfort. This hardwiring tunes us in to the sensational, the dramatic, and to the expression of emotion by others.[25]

This chapter gives you tools to leverage the power of familiarity and emotion when presenting in business. These tools will help your information "filter through" to your listeners' minds and hearts. You will be more compelling and improve your listeners' abilities to understand and remember your information. Both you and your listeners will have more fun.

Repetition

Repetition is the simplest way to leverage one of the two keys to long-term memory: the power of familiarity. It reinforces information and improves the chance that listeners will remember it.

Everything is new the first time you hear it. The second time it may "sound familiar." The third time, you welcome it with a satisfying feeling: "Yes, I know that." The fourth time the response is something like "Again? This must be important."

Now factor this in: Not everybody is listening closely every moment. The chances are good that they will miss some information. They may miss it twice!

Many presenters resist repeating information because they fear the audience will be bored or impatient. It takes time—time they could use to say more or add greater detail. If you want listeners to walk away remembering your most important points, limit the amount of detail and repeat those points at least three times. If it is worth remembering, it is worth repeating.

How can you do this? The classic approach is to say it in your opening or content preview, say it again in the body of your presentation, and say it once more when you review or close. There are other ways you can use the power of repetition. To say something not just more than once but also in more than one way is a great way to reinforce a message. This makes important points more familiar, more emotional, more effective, more fun to hear, and much more likely to be remembered.

Transitions

A transition is used to move from one section of your presentation to the next. Often, speakers have a sense that transitions are helpful, but they can't quite say why. Transitions, like landmarks on a long journey, confirm that you are on course. They show how far you have come and how far you still have to go. They answer the questions "Where are we? Why are we going this way? How much longer till we get there?" Transitions emphasize the connections between the different elements in your talk and make it easier for the audience to understand how different elements combine to make the "big picture." Consider these examples from a presentation about gardening.

Transitions tell:

- *What you have covered:* "So now you know how to prepare the soil."

- *Why you covered it*: "Again, soil preparation is important. It encourages strong and healthy plants."

- *What you will cover next:* "Now let's talk about how to transplant the seedlings into the prepared soil."

- *Why you will cover it:* "Follow these next tips to transplant successfully. Your seedlings will grow like weeds!"

- *Connections between the two points covered:* "Again, remember to think backwards. The type of seedling determines the type of soil preparation."

- *Connections between the two points and a larger whole:* "As with every aspect of gardening, patience is the key. Remember: plan, prepare, plant, have patience. Nature will do the rest."

Still, too many sound verbose or pedantic. Use the types of transitions your audience needs. Here are some tips to help you decide when transitions are valuable.

- *Transitions Help with Long Presentations.* On a fifty-minute flight from Los Angeles to San Francisco, it may not matter when you fly over Fresno. On a five-hour flight from New York to L.A., it is nice to be able to track your flight path on the video screen.

- *A Long Pause Can Be Used as a Transition.* Transitions should not be used to prevent silence. A presentation without pauses is like a paragraph without punctuation (commas, periods, etc.). Just as that paragraph is hard to read, that type of speech makes it difficult to listen to and difficult to understand, assign value to, or respond intellectually or emotionally to. A healthy pause may be the only transition you need.

- *Try a Brief Question-and-Answer Session at Transition Points.* Intermittent question-and-answer sessions can add or clarify information. This helps your listeners better understand the information that follows, which is especially useful in technical, scientific, and educational presentations. Intermittent question-and-answer sessions give highly analytical listeners a chance to clear up any unresolved issues that might otherwise nag at them and distract them as you move on. The questions will give you a better sense of your listeners' concerns. Then you can tailor your information to them. Finally, it can be a nice change of pace.

Quotations

Quotations make you and your message more credible. When you use a quotation to support your position, that position immediately becomes much more than your opinion. Quoting an authority respected by the audience immediately gives you an "expert witness."

Great quotations capture the essence of an idea in a sound bite. A quotation can reinforce your point and make it more memorable. Humorous quotations can lighten a somber mood. Quotations can give a sense of history and hope by showing that a problem has been faced and overcome in the past.

Whatever is well said by another is mine.
SENECA

The Internet is a rich source of quotations. There are many books of quotations in any bookstore, including collections of quotations from business leaders, humorous quotations, and quotations specially selected for public speakers. Once you find that perfect quotation, follow these guidelines to use it most effectively.

Using Quotations

These suggestions will help you deliver quotations for maximum effectiveness.

- *Be brief.* Less is more. Quote only the key or relevant words or passages. An overly detailed explanation of the background or context can make the quotation anticlimactic.

- *Get it right.* If quoting directly, feel free to make a written note of the exact words and to read it aloud to the audience. Don't risk forgetting or misquoting. Remember that your memory may be temporarily unreliable due to the stress of delivering a presentation.

- *Attribute it accurately.* Give due credit—and give it to the right source. When a U.S. Secretary of Education attributed a quotation to the wrong Greek philosopher, that was the only part of his talk widely quoted in the press.

- *Distinguish between direct and indirect quotations.* If you don't know the original, guess only if you acknowledge you are guessing. If the person you quote is extremely well-known to your audience, an explanation of who that person is (or was) is not necessary.

- *Consider sharing the context.* Telling when, where, or why the quote originated may enrich the meaning of the quote. Was the original speaker facing an enormous challenge, showing admirable strength or courage, or speaking from a wealth of experience?

- *"Sandwich" the quotation in pauses.* Pause before you deliver the actual quote to create anticipation. Pause again after the quotation to let the meaning sink in.

- *Speak slowly and clearly.* Use the appropriate inflection. Reading a quotation can be the best way to make sure you deliver the quotation accurately.

- *Return to your topic.* Use a key word or phrase from the quotation to reinforce the link between the quotation and your point.

To use quotations skillfully, practice using the three steps that follow. As Cicero wrote, "The skill to do is in the doing."

1. Supply any needed credit and context.

2. Deliver the quotation.

3. Link the quotation back to the topic at hand.

Here is an example using the three steps.

Step 1. In a case brought before the Supreme Court, a writer for *The New Yorker* magazine claimed a constitutional right to make up quotations as long as the writer believes they reflect the views of the subject. Although many journalists do not agree with the practice, it does reflect an acknowledgment of the power of quotations to provide authority and a sense of authenticity. In a ruling on the case, Federal Appeals Judge Alex Kozinski wrote,

There are two ways of spreading light: to be the candle or the mirror that reflects it.

EDITH WHARTON

Step 2. "An article devoid of (quotations), one that consists entirely of the author's own observations and conclusions, generally leaves readers dissatisfied and unpersuaded as well as bored."[26]

Step 3. If you want to increase your ability to satisfy and persuade your listeners, use a pertinent quotation from a respected source.

Comparisons

Comparisons help listeners understand and appreciate numbers and statistics. Compare these three ways of stating the size and population of Alaska.

1. Alaska covers 570,000 square miles. It has about 750,000 residents.

2. The state of Alaska has 750,000 residents in 570,000 square miles. The city of San Francisco has 750,000 residents in 49 square miles.

3. Alaska covers 570,000 square miles. That is as big as the 26 states east of the Mississippi River combined. It has about 750,000 residents, the same as the city of San Francisco—not including the rest of the Bay area.

Both numbers two and three will have more impact than number one.

Comparative Images

You can also leverage the power of comparison by creating a comparative image a listener can easily visualize.

- All the groundwater, lakes, and rivers in the world, added to all the water in Earth's atmosphere, make up only 0.0015 percent of the earth's water. This is equivalent to a quarter of a teaspoon drinking water added to a bathtub full of saltwater.[27]

- The moon is almost as wide as Australia, about a quarter as wide as the earth.[28]

> **We hear and apprehend only what we already half know.**
> HENRY THOREAU

Analogies, Metaphors, and Similes

When we hear "It's a lot like" or "That reminds me of," we hear the tendency of the human mind to look for similarities and connections. The use of an analogy, metaphor, or simile makes our information more understandable and memorable. It uses the already familiar to make the listener more comfortable with new information. It also makes it easier for our listeners to explain the point to a third party.

Analogies, metaphors, and similes help explain or illustrate a concept. They take advantage of a listener's current knowledge and understanding to help them understand the abstract, the complex, and the new more quickly and more deeply. Because they start with the familiar, they help your listeners feel more comfortable with new information.

In *The Unfolding of Language*, linguist Dr. Guy Deutscher explains, "Metaphor is an essential tool of thought, an indispensable conceptual mechanism which allows us to think of abstract notions in terms of simpler, concrete things. It is, in fact, the only way we have of dealing with abstraction."[29]

The Differences Between Analogies, Metaphors, and Similes

An analogy is a comparison that shows the similarity between two things in one or more ways, and describes the ways in which they resemble one another. They can be used to infer that if two things are alike in one respect, they must be alike in others.

Life is not having been told that the man has just waxed the floor.

OGDEN NASH

A metaphor is a figure of speech used to suggest a resemblance between two things that aren't truly alike. "Life is a journey" and "love is a battlefield" are metaphors. A simile also points out a similarity but does it more directly, usually using the words *like* or *as*. "Falling in love is like going to war" is a simile.

There is some gray area between comparisons, analogies, metaphors, and similes. The finer points aside, what is important is the way you can use these figures of speech to make your content more understandable and memorable.

Form, Function, and Feeling

Analogies, metaphors, and similes often point out a similarity in form, function, or feeling.

- Form: a network of suppliers

- Function: a corporate whistle-blower

- Feeling: a wet blanket on the mood

Analogies, Metaphors, and Similes Must Tap an Existing Knowledge Base

Analogies must do more than just point out how one thing is like another. Understanding the existing knowledge base of your listeners and choosing an analogy that will leverage part of that knowledge base are key to using an effective analogy. If your listener is familiar with neither, the analogy won't work.

Fresh Analogies, Metaphors, and Similes

A fresh, unexpected similarity in the form, function, or feeling of two otherwise dissimilar things can be refreshing. It may need a brief explanation as to why the comparison was made—why and how the speaker believes the two things are similar. Consider this explanation by Elisabeth Kübler-Ross: "People are like stained glass windows. They sparkle and shine when the sun is out, but when the darkness sets in, their true beauty is revealed only if there is a light from within."[30]

Kübler-Ross included several comparisons. In addition to "people are like stained glass windows" she used "darkness" to mean adversity and disappointment, and "light" to mean strength of character that includes perseverance and optimism. The listener supplies the understanding, and, because Kübler-Ross established the overriding analogy, the unspoken comparisons honor one's ability to complete the picture.

Dr. Paula Hammond, head of MIT's Department of Chemical Engineering—in her eleven-minute TED talk, A New Superweapon in the Fight Against Cancer—uses fun, familiar, and effective metaphors to describe the nanotechnology she and her colleagues developed to fight drug-resistant cancers. She describes their engineered set of cancer-fighting molecules as a "superweapon" in an "invisibility cloak" deployed against a "supervillain with incredible superpowers."

"We have to target this superweapon to the supervillain cells that reside in the tumor.... We have to sneak our nanoparticle past the tumor defense system...by disguising it. So we add one more...layer around this nanoparticle...a cloud of water molecules around the nanoparticle that gives us an invisibility cloaking effect. This invisibility cloak allows the nanoparticle to travel through the bloodstream...to reach the tumor..."[31]

In a twelve–minute TED talk, multiple-award-winning geneticist Dr. Jennifer Doudna of the University of California, Berkeley, used at least seven: a ticking time bomb, a sentinel, a cleaver, a scissors, computer hardwiring, programmable software, and a vaccination card.[32]

This passage is from a TED talk by Wade

The key instrument of the creative imagination is analogy.
EDWARD O. WILSON

Davis, multitalented anthropologist, biologist, ethnographer, writer, photographer, and filmmaker.

"Now, together the myriad cultures of the world make up a web of spiritual life and cultural life that envelops the planet, and is as important to the well-being of the planet as indeed is the biological web of life that you know as a biosphere. And you might think of this cultural web of life as being an ethnosphere, and you might define the ethnosphere as being the sum total of all thoughts and dreams, myths, ideas, inspirations, intuitions brought into being by the human imagination since the dawn of consciousness. The ethnosphere is humanity's great legacy. It's the symbol of all that we are and all that we can be as an astonishingly inquisitive species.

"And just as the biosphere has been severely eroded, so too is the ethnosphere—and, if anything, at a far greater rate. No biologists, for example, would dare suggest that 50 percent of all species or more have been or are on the brink of extinction because it simply is not true, and yet that—the most apocalyptic scenario in the realm of biological diversity—scarcely approaches what we know to be the most optimistic scenario in the realm of cultural diversity. And the great indicator of that, of course, is language loss.

"When each of you in this room were born, there were 6,000 languages spoken on the planet. Now, a language is not just a body of vocabulary or a set of grammatical rules. A language is a flash of the human spirit. It's a vehicle through which the soul of each particular culture comes into the material world. Every language is an old-growth forest of the mind, a watershed, a thought, an ecosystem of spiritual possibilities. And of those 6,000 languages, as we sit here today…fully half are no longer being whispered into the ears of children."[33]

Cluster Carefully

Notice the cluster of metaphors in the closing paragraph above, metaphors that reinforce the use of the listener's understanding of biosphere to then understand Davis' concept of an ethnosphere. Done in this way, skillfully, clustering can be powerful as well as poetic. Yet, more than one image used to support a single idea can muddy the water. Consider the confusion of images in this statement: "Our entire team is facing an uphill battle on rough terrain in the months ahead. We will have to navigate some stormy seas before we can land safely."

Everything must be like something, so what is this like?

E.M. FORSTER

Say what? A team (sports) is battling (military, on a hill) to navigate stormy seas (a ship, a storm at sea) before they can land (an airplane). This does not work well.

Business Analogies, Metaphors, and Similes

These are a dime a dozen. Why? Because they bring to mind an image that people can relate to, an image that evokes emotion or drama or glamour. The following are familiar, and not exhaustive in any of the categories. Some are so familiar as to have become clichés. The point here is that they were effective. They got the job done and stood the test of time. Here are some common business analogies, and phrases that refer to them.

Business Is War

Join forces, rally the troops, armed with information, run it up the flagpole, the chain of command, outflank the competition, marketing campaign, give marching orders, the smell of blood, gain ground, lose ground, battle for success, bring out the big guns, take no prisoners

Business Is Sport

Kickoff meeting, team player, get the ball rolling, keep your eye on the ball, the ball is in your court, score big, tackle a problem, level the playing field, cover the bases, jump hurdles, hit a home run, hit it out of the park, it's a slam dunk, get ahead, fall behind, raise the bar, land a big one, take the gloves off, take it on the chin, hitting below the belt, throw in the towel, in the home stretch, cross the finish line

Business Is Farming

Seed money, plant seeds, cross-pollinate workers, a tough row to hoe, prune the staff, cut out dead wood, seasonal markets, branch out, branch office, buy the farm, low-hanging fruit, ripe for the picking, come to fruition, reap the rewards

Business Is Gambling

Don't show your cards, keep it close to the vest, put your cards on the table, roll the dice, stack the deck, it's a crap shoot, play the cards you're dealt, keep a poker face, an underhanded deal, throw in your cards

Business Is Driving

Step on the gas, put the pedal to the metal, get up to speed, firing on all cylinders, spin your wheels, stuck in neutral, take a detour, hit a dead end, blow a gasket, hit the brakes, come to a screeching stop

Technical Terms Prove the Power of Analogies, Metaphors, and Similes

Dr. Deutscher refers to language, using the metaphor of a coral reef as "a reef of dead metaphor." He shows how many modern words and word usages originated as metaphors although we no longer recognize them as such. To understand the human tendency to explain the more complex or abstract in terms of metaphor, and the way these metaphors evolve into everyday terms, look at what has happened in the last few decades. Metaphors have eased us into a more complex, abstraction-rich, technical world. Many metaphoric computer and technology terms have become so much a part of our everyday life that we don't even think about earlier meanings when we use them.

Consider these terms: *bit, boot, bug, chip, clipboard, cloud, cookie, crash, dashboard, desktop, dock, document, driver, export, file, firewall, folder, hardware, icon, import, keyboard, link, mouse, network, password, portal, tab, virus, web.*

Apple took the edge off the word "computer."

STEVE JOBS

Common terms were chosen because they were, in some way, similar to a new technology. They made new technologies faster and easier to understand and use, and easy to remember. They made them less intimidating.

When you want your information to be understood more easily and quickly, and be remembered, analogies, metaphors, and similarities can be just the tool you need to get the job done.

Use four steps to create your own analogy.

Start with the point you want to make, and then introduce the analogy to help explain or reinforce it. Fresh analogies, new ways of looking at things, are always more interesting, but you do need to analogize to something within your listeners' existing knowledge base.

Step 1. State the point clearly and briefly. Edit the point to one sentence.

Example:

"In modern languages, the meanings and usages of words and phrases often originated as metaphors."

Step 2. Include facts and essential details.

Example:

"Familiar terms are used as metaphors to help explain things that are more abstract. Many computer and technology terms are so much a part of our everyday life that we don't even remember they began as metaphors.

"Consider these terms: bit, bug, chip, clipboard, crash, dashboard, desktop, dock, document, export, file, firewall, folder, hardware, icon, import, keyboard, link, mouse, network, password, portal, tab, virus, web.

"Common terms were chosen because they were, in some way, similar to a new technology. These terms made new technologies faster and easier to understand and use, easy to remember, and less intimidating."

Step 3. Introduce and develop the analogy. Explain why and how this is an analogy. Are the two things similar in form, function, or feeling? The metaphor that follows is taken word for word from the conclusion of Dr. Deutscher's work on language as metaphor.

Example:

"Like a reef, which grows from layer upon layer of dead coral skeletons, new structures in language can rise from the layers of dead metaphors deposited by the flow towards abstraction."[34]

Step 4. Repeat the point. Reinforce your position.

Example:

"When you want your information to be understood more easily and quickly, and be remembered, build a reef. Use analogies, metaphors, and similarities to get the job done."

Here are the same sentences, as they would flow during a presentation.

"In modern languages, the meanings and usages of words and phrases often originated as metaphors. Familiar terms are used as metaphors to help explain things that are more abstract. Many computer and technology terms are so much a part of our everyday life that we don't even remember they began as metaphors.

"Consider these terms: bit, bug, chip, clipboard, crash, dashboard, desktop, dock, document, export, file, firewall, folder, hardware, icon, import, keyboard, link, mouse, network, password, portal, tab, virus, web.

"Common terms were chosen because they were, in some way, similar to a new technology. These terms made new technologies faster and easier to understand and use, easy to remember, and less intimidating."

Analogies, it is true, decide nothing, but they can make one feel more at home.

SIGMUND FREUD

"'Like a reef, which grows from layer upon layer of dead coral skeletons, new structures in language can rise from the layers of dead metaphors deposited by the flow towards abstraction.'[35]

"When you want your information to be understood more easily and quickly, and be remembered, build a reef. Use analogies, metaphors, and similarities to get the job done."

Stories

Stories, legends, fables, myths, yarns, anecdotes, tales, chronicles. We love stories. Long before humans could read or write, we listened to and told stories. Stories teach, inspire, caution, and help us remember. They define who we are and who we want to be. The right story at the right time shows an understanding of the listener's needs and concerns.

Use Stories to Influence Others

The skillful use of stories can be enormously helpful in influencing others. In the words of Annette Simmons, author of *The Story Factor—The Secrets of Influence from the Art of Storytelling*:

> "Before you attempt to influence anyone, you need to establish enough trust to successfully deliver your message… Since you don't usually have time to build trust based on personal experience, the best you can do is tell them a story that simulates an experience of your trustworthiness. Hearing your story is as close as they can get to firsthand experience of watching you 'walk the walk' as opposed to 'talk the talk.' A story lets them decide for themselves—one of the great secrets of true influence… People value their own conclusions more than they value yours… If your story is good enough, people—of their own free will—come to the conclusion they can trust you and the message you bring."[36]

Simmons identifies six types of stories that are useful when you need to influence or persuade your audience:

1. "Who I Am" stories

2. "Values-In-Action" stories

3. "Why I Am Here" stories

4. "Teaching" stories

5. "The Vision" stories

6. "I Know What You Are Thinking" stories[37]

Stories Are a Powerful Management Tool

Stories can be a wonderful tool for influencing behavior. Here's why:

- *Stories have universal appeal.* Stories appeal to sophisticated as well as less sophisticated listeners. Everyone loves a good story. Choose an appropriate story, and tailor the telling to your audience. Stories are timeless, not a passing fad.

- *Stories communicate values and traditions.* The stories a company generates tell when customer service is the first priority, when innovation is valued over obedience, when the mission statement is lived or only mouthed. They implicitly teach people how to behave.

- *Stories are natural and powerful training tools.* In teaching people how to behave, stories teach ways to solve problems, when and how to ask for help, or when to make an on-the-spot decision to solve a production problem or satisfy a customer.[38]

- *Stories recognize and reward effort and achievement.* The stories behind the high ratings in a personnel file can be shared to encourage more of the same. Instead of waiting to tell stories when the gold watch is given, or losing both the story and the great performer to a competitor, sharing success stories in whatever way possible will breed more of the same.

- *Stories are fun and memorable.* Tell a good story and it will live for a long, long time. Many of those who hear it told will tell it again, spreading the word for you, and learning the lessons of the story again each time they tell it.[39]

> **Nothing serves a leader better than a knack for narrative. Stories appoint role models, impart values, and show how to execute indescribably complex tasks.**
> THOMAS A. STEWART

Using Stories Effectively

Keep stories short. Stories work best when they last less than two minutes. More than that and you risk boring the audience or having them resent the valuable time you take before you "get to the point." It is a good idea to do a script of the story, time your delivery, and if over two minutes, edit it to essential details only. The journalist's approach of answering who, what, when, where, and why can help you trim excess detail. Anything else is likely to be a detail that could be cut.

Consciously choose a current or classic story. If you want to make a point about a new issue, or show how your subject relates to a changing environment, a contemporary story or stories may be best. If you want to teach an enduring lesson or show that an issue is recurring, a more classic or historical story may work best.

In his autobiography, *As It Happened*, William Paley, founder of CBS, uses a historical story to make an enduring point. He tells how in the early days of radio in the 1930s, he used the perception of CBS as the underdog to his advantage. It is especially interesting because he recounts the value of telling a story, with its powerful analogy, to persuade advertisers to sponsor programs on CBS.

In the early days, NBC was more prestigious than Paley's CBS. NBC had more money, more people, and fancier offices and studios. The perception of CBS as the underdog made it difficult for Paley to persuade advertisers to buy airtime, even though he believed CBS had better programs. He writes, "It caused me considerable anguish until one day my whole attitude of being the perpetual underdog changed."

Walking one day in New York City, he passed the Capitol Theater, the largest, most luxurious movie theater in town. Across the street he noticed a shabby theater. But the shabby theater had a long line in front! It struck him that people would patronize an ordinary, even shabby theater to see the best movie. "The analogy struck me so forcibly that I never forgot it... The radio listener doesn't know what kind of office I have, what kind of studios I have, he only knows what he hears. And I can forget about all these advantages my competition has... I just have to put things on the air that the people will like more."

Paley began to tell that story to potential advertisers. The result? "That story became a very strong point in my being able to persuade advertisers to sponsor programs on CBS. That insight affected me, too, for I became extra careful about spending money on anything in the company that did not affect the product, the program itself."[40]

Cluster Stories

David Pogue, personal technology columnist, tech correspondent, and author, tells three quick stories, one firsthand and two secondhand, in his TED Talk *Simplicity Sells*.

> I once had the distinct privilege of sitting in on the Apple call center for a day. The guy had a duplicate headset for me to listen to. And the calls that—you know how they say, "Your

call may be recorded for quality assurance"? Uh-uh. Your call may be recorded so that they can collect the funniest dumb user stories and pass them around on a CD.

Which they do. (Laughter)

And I have a copy. (Laughter)

It's in your gift bag. No, no. With your voices on it! (Laughter)

So, some of the stories are just so classic, and yet so understandable. A woman called Apple to complain that her mouse was squeaking. Making a squeaking noise.

And the technician said, "Well, ma'am, what do you mean your mouse is squeaking?"

She says, "All I can tell you is that it squeaks louder, the faster I move it across the screen." (Laughter)

And the technician's like, "Ma'am, you've got the mouse up against the screen?"

She goes, "Well, the message said, 'Click here to continue.'" (Laughter)

Well, if you like that one—how much time have we got? Another one, a guy called—this is absolutely true—his computer had crashed, and he told the technician he couldn't restart it, no matter how many times he typed "11."

And the technician said, "What? Why are you typing 11?"

He said, "The message says, 'Error Type 11.'"

(Laughter)

> **Good storytelling is harder to do than it sounds, but the easy part is that everyone has the ability to do it.**
>
> PETER GUBER

So, we must admit that some of the blame falls squarely at the feet of the users. But why is the technical overload crisis, the complexity crisis, accelerating now?[41]

Plan Your Story

Use the following steps to plan and edit your story. This is vitally important in order to tell it well without rambling or missing important details.

Step 1: *Tell the story.* Start strong without a preamble such as "Now I'm going to tell you a little story that helps illustrate my point." Instead, dive in. As soon as you start, the listeners will know you are telling a story. This is the adult version of "Once upon a time…" It might begin with "The summer before his sophomore year in college, my son Jack decided to take his car to school. In mid-August, he packed it up and left Los Angeles, heading for Boston."

Step 2: *When you finish the story, state the point you want to make.* State it clearly and succinctly. Notice how in the stories used as examples, both William Paley and David Pogue clearly stated the point of their stories when they finished. This is important to do, as stories will otherwise mean different things to different listeners. When you tell a story, you have the right and responsibility to decide and state the point.

What is the moral or lesson the story teaches? What is the principle it illustrates? Is it the importance of teamwork? Patience? Perseverance? Creativity? Following the rules? Regular maintenance? The story of Jack might have a concluding point that sounds something like this: "Now Jack gets an oil change exactly as often as recommended."

Step 3: *Introduce the related topic or issue, and state how the point or principle illustrated by the story applies.* If you want to sell a maintenance service package, state the importance of regular maintenance to the cost of repairs and downtime. After the story about Jack, the related topic could be "Just as with a car, regular inspections and maintenance are absolutely critical with production equipment like yours."

Step 4: *Develop the topic or issue at hand.* For example, explain what the maintenance service package will include, describe the problems it will prevent, discuss how it can be customized, and estimate the overall cost savings to the potential buyer. Although no mention of the story is needed in this step, the information you cover here prepares you to reinforce your point with support from the story.

Step 5: *Close the discussion of the issue by using a brief reference back to the story.* "So just as Jack's regular oil changes now help make sure he won't find himself stuck in the Mojave Desert with a melting engine, regular maintenance of your production equipment will help it run smoothly, dependably, and very profitably, for many years to come."

Can a story be as thrilling as the biggest and most expensive ride in the history of SeaWorld? Here's what James Zoltak, editor of *Amusement Business* magazine says about SeaWorld San Diego's mega-million-dollar Journey to Atlantis ride: "Story is really what captures people's imaginations, as much as the adrenaline aspects of a thrill ride. Experts I've heard talk about attraction development have said storytelling is one of the most important aspects, right along with ride systems and other effects."[42]

The Journey to Atlantis ride at SeaWorld lasts six minutes, twenty-three seconds. The story of the lost continent of Atlantis has been told and re-told for three thousand years.

> **Narration is as much a part of human nature as breath and the circulation of the blood…storytelling is intrinsic to biological time, which we cannot escape.**
>
> A.S. BYATT

Humor

The ability to use humor well is a wonderful asset. It can help the speaker make a point, connect with listeners emotionally, and lighten the mood. Humor creates a sense of community. But humor can be risky. When an attempt to be funny fails, it can fail in a big way. It can fall flat or, worse, offend or alienate your listeners.

Dr. Richard Wiseman of the University of Hertfordshire designed an experiment to determine the World's Funniest Joke. Ten thousand volunteers from eleven countries were invited to judge jokes and contribute their own. From over forty thousand jokes and two million ratings, here is an abridged version of the one elected the World's Funniest Joke.

> Two hunters are out in the woods when one of them collapses, lies prostrate, eyes glazed over, and doesn't seem to be breathing. The other hunter takes out his phone and calls 911.
>
> He gasps, "My friend is dead! What can I do?" The operator says, "Calm down, I can help. First, let's make sure he's dead." There is a silence; then a gunshot is heard.
>
> "Okay," the hunter says, "now what?"

You probably smiled or chuckled after reading this, but is it really the funniest joke you ever heard? Chances are that it is not. Most of us have been reduced to helpless, breathless, doubled-over laughter at some point in our lives. And most of us, when trying to relate the humor of the moment to others later, have been reduced to saying, "Well, I guess you had to be there."

Robert Benchley said, "Examining humor seriously is like dissecting a frog. There's nothing funny about it, and the subject dies in the process." Yet we can examine the nature of humor and come to some conclusions about what makes something tickle the human funny bone.

Humor Creates a Sense of Community

Ted Cohen, professor of philosophy at the University of Chicago, explains that when we tell a joke, we presuppose something in those who listen—some knowledge, belief, familiarity, or prejudice—that will supply the background needed for the joke to succeed. Whether very simple or very complex, the joke will always require the audience to supply something. When members of an audience supply that something simultaneously, a community is created—a community

> There's nothing like a gleam of humor to reassure you that a fellow human being is ticking inside a strange face.
>
> EVA HOFFMAN

of people joined by the understanding of what they share with the joke teller and with each other.[43]

These guidelines will help you use humor effectively.

- *Make it quick.* The more you draw out a joke, the more you raise the expectations of your audience. Get to the punch line quickly. People need to see the humor themselves. The slow build-up of expectations can make them feel manipulated.

- *Pause to let the laughter happen.* Laughter is contagious, and humor works best when people laugh together, out loud. Stop after a funny line. Let people enjoy the moment. Don't stifle the laughter by talking again too soon.

- *Be cautious about humor aimed at an individual or group.* Aristotle taught that all humor was at the expense of someone. Be careful not to offend an individual, members of a group, or a person who may have sympathy with others.

- *Make it relevant.* Telling a joke just to "warm up the audience" can smack of manipulation. Instead, choose humor that makes or supports a point from your presentation. Even if not everyone thinks it is funny, at least they will see the point, which means you haven't wasted their time.

- *Use a touch of self-directed humor.* When we can poke fun at ourselves and take ourselves lightly, it can create the impression of extreme confidence. It can demonstrate a willingness to learn from our mistakes, and to consider the ideas and opinions of others.

- *Avoid too much self-deprecating humor.* Reciting a list of your mistakes can make you seem like a slow learner. Avoid humor so consistently self-deprecating that the audience begins to believe you have a low opinion of yourself.

- *Be sensitive to the pain often inherent in humor.* Much humor has a basis in discomfort or pain. If the audience is likely to be highly sensitive, the pain is too great or simply too recent, the attempt at humor may seem insensitive and in bad taste.

- *Use humor that is funny to the audience in general, not to just a few members.* Consider whether audience members have the background to fill in the necessary information to see the humor. If the humor depends on familiarity with a quirk of language or knowledge of a historical event significant to only one group of people, it may not work well with a diverse audience.

A joke is a very serious thing.
WINSTON CHURCHILL

Summary

In this world of information overload, we have all learned to filter out most of what we hear and focus only on what matters to us. This means that most of what we say in presentations will be briefly considered by our listeners and then forgotten. What is remembered after the presentations? Information that has one or both of these two qualities:

1. It evokes emotion in the listener.

2. It is somehow familiar, somehow connected to something the listener already knows.

The tools covered in this chapter have stood the test of time for making information more compelling and memorable. Use them and your message will rise above the white noise of information overload.

Repetition is the simplest way to leverage the power of familiarity. It reinforces information and improves the chance that your listeners will remember what you said.

Transitions can leverage the familiar by repeating or referencing an important point. They can emphasize the connection between points and help the listener understand how points combine to make the big picture.

Quotations add credibility by showing that your point is more than your opinion. They give a sense of history and hope by showing others have faced a similar problem. Humorous quotations help lighten a somber mood, put things in a different perspective, and give your listeners a sound bite to remember and repeat.

Comparisons, analogies, metaphors, and similes take advantage of the familiar. They leverage your listener's current knowledge and understanding and make new, complex, or conceptual information understandable. Because they start with the familiar, they make listeners more comfortable with new information. Using comparisons is a great way to help listeners understand and appreciate numbers and statistics.

Stories and anecdotes tap into your listener's emotions and help them recall similar or related experiences. Stories are a powerful way to influence and persuade. When remembered and retold by listeners, they carry your message to a wider audience. The points or lessons of the story are made again and again.

Humor taps into some unspoken but shared knowledge, emotion, or pain to create a sense of community. It changes the pace, lightens the mood, and helps present you as human.

These creative ways of presenting your content help you rise above the noise of information overload. By using them to evoke emotion and leverage the power of the familiar, your content will be more meaningful, memorable, and enjoyable.

7

PICTURE THIS

Visual Aids That Really Are

Good visual aids should aid the audience by making it easier to pay attention, understand, and remember. If that does not happen, if visual aids do not help (aid) the audience members by giving them something to look at (a visual), they did not *visually aid* them and do not deserve the name.

Hearing information involves only one of the five senses; the use of visual aids adds one more and creates a richer overall experience. The old sayings "Seeing is believing" and "A picture is worth a thousand words" testify to the value of visual aids.

Yet we have all sat through presentations in which the "visual aids" were so ineffective, they didn't deserve the name. They were boring. They were too simplistic to add value. They were too detailed to process. They couldn't be seen.

It is good to remember that for many centuries speakers did not use anything like the visual aids we use today. The most memorable speeches throughout history were made without them. Not only is it possible to speak without visual aids, sometimes it is better.

This seems almost heresy in some environments, especially in many corporations where electronic slides rule the day. Sadly, many classroom teachers, even in the elementary grades, dim the lights, put up a slide, and begin to talk. This may work in some situations, but certainly not in all. So, let's first consider when and when not to use visual aids. The guidelines below will help you make wise choices.

Do use visual elements to:

- Illustrate hard-to-visualize information

- Evoke emotion

- Help explain relationships

- Help assign value

- Help the audience remember

- Stimulate interest

- Focus attention

Do not use visual elements to:

- Serve as detailed speaker notes

- Present simple ideas that are easily stated verbally

- Impress your audience with quantity of detail

- Prove how many PowerPoint features you can use

- Avoid interaction with the audience

When a visual element—a chart, graph, photograph, and so on—cannot be removed without harming comprehension, it is germane. If it can be eliminated at no cost *to the listeners*, it is not serving the listeners well. Remove it.

Visual Aids Are Not Speaker Notes

The dos and don'ts above should lead to this conclusion: Your speaker notes are unlikely to make good visual aids, and vice versa. If your notes are comprehensive, they will probably include more detail, or different forms of detail, than should be included on a visual aid. If you use slides as your only speaker notes, you must be ruthless in editing out those things best communicated verbally.

It may help to have notes to yourself that the audience cannot see. A reminder to give an example, tell a story, summarize before moving on, repeat something slowly, ask a rhetorical question, or reminders about how to handle logistical or facilities issues (for example, when to show a slide, when to turn the lights back on, or when to call for a break). These things belong in speaker notes, not in visual aids.

In Chapter 1 you learned how the normal stress of delivering a presentation could cause a cortisol-induced memory lapse, and that our brains are not designed to remember scripts easily. There is no way you can be sure you will remember everything you plan to say or do without checking speaker notes during your presentation. So use notes. Chapter 4 helps you make good notes. Chapter 12 teaches you to use notes with confidence.

When you can clearly separate, in your mind and in your media, the difference between speaker notes and visual aids, you can decide if you really need visual aids. If so, the following advice will help you use them well.

Choose the Best Type of Visual Aids

Choose based on the topic, the venue, the availability of equipment, and your own preferences. Often the choice is obvious. If you have flexibility, choose the simplest option appropriate for the occasion and venue. Flipcharts, whiteboards, chalkboards, actual product samples, demonstrations, videos, and other types can be appropriate.

Many of the following design guidelines will apply to a wide variety of visual aids. Because of their prevalence in today's world, these guidelines will focus on electronic slides.

Computer-Generated Slides

Two leading applications for creating and using computer-generated slides are PowerPoint and Keynote. Most of the functions on these two programs are the same, and a presentation developed in one can usually be safely shown on the other application. Keynote does have a few methods of animation that do not translate to PowerPoint, so if you plan to create a presentation in Keynote and use it in PowerPoint, it is best to stick with the basic animation functions and run it in PowerPoint to check that it all works as designed before you use it in front of an audience.

Slides give tremendous flexibility and convenience in both design and use. Many organizations have a design template. The template creates a consistent look, and usually includes the company's logo and signature colors for a professional look. Presentation software always includes a number of standard templates. Use of a standard template may eliminate the need to consider the following principles. But if you can design slides, consider the following guidelines.

Color

Color is powerful. Used well, it clarifies and accelerates understanding of your information and increases emotional impact. Use color to highlight important information, to establish hierarchies of information, and to group related points. Used well, color makes your message look more professional and polished. Use it to achieve these goals, not just for decoration.

Color affects us. Everyone should have a paint box and a large box of crayons.

DR. SUNWOLF

Contrast Is Vital

Color contrast is key. Different colors may not give the contrast you need. When the value of two colors (the relative darkness or lightness) is about the same, the line between the background and the text can be hard to see. The text may look fuzzy around the edges or may appear to move or vibrate. To check if the values of colors are different enough to work well together, look at them in gray scale. If the contrast is not easy to see in gray scale, it may not be easy to see in color.

Consider a Deep Blue or Green Background

Given a choice of natural environments, people gravitate toward blue and green. The most coveted real estate in the world offers views with both, and those who can afford them choose views of oceans, lakefronts, rivers, and parks. Blue and green ultimately sustain life on Earth. Multiple award-winning scientist and conservationist Edward O. Wilson calls this human affinity for the natural world *biophilia*.[44] Deep blue or green backgrounds leverage this human preference. And the leading favorite color, chosen by 40 percent of people polled, is blue.

Avoid White Backgrounds

Looking at a series of slides with white or very light backgrounds is like staring at a snowfield on a sunny day—not easy on the eyes! Light backgrounds are great for printed material but not for a lit screen.

White or Yellow Text

White as the basic text color and yellow for emphasis is a common and effective choice. Very light shades of other colors can work well. Choose colors that provide high contrast with your background.

Color Vision Deficiency

People with color vision deficiency (color blindness) cannot distinguish certain colors. Estimates of the percentage of the population with color deficiency usually range between 8 and 12 percent of males and half of 1 percent of females. About 99 percent of cases involve red/green color blindness. Blue/yellow color vision deficiency is rare, and total color blindness (seeing in only shades of gray) is extremely rare.[45] You may want to minimize the amount of red and green you use, especially if they have the same value.

Text Guidelines for Visual Aids

Font Size

Make all text large enough to read easily. Text size may vary with the sizes of your screen and audience. Fewer words make larger fonts possible. Generally accepted minimum guidelines are twenty-point text with thirty-point text for titles, but consider the size of your audience and screen. Bigger is usually better.

Clean and Simple Fonts Work Best

Arial is a top choice for slide fonts. It is a sans serif font, clean and simple with no little artifacts at the end of the character points. It also has an extended font family—Arial Narrow, Arial Black, Arial Rounded MT Bold (Figure 7.1). You can add variety without creating an entirely new look. It works well across platforms. Remember, even within the same font family, more than two varieties of text can be distracting.

Table 7.1 The Arial Font Family

The Arial Family

This is Arial, a simple sans serif font.

This is Arial italicized.

This is Arial Narrow.

This is Arial Bold.

This is Arial Black.

This is Arial Rounded MT Bold.

Avoid Using All Capitals

All capitals are harder—hence slower—to read. They also make it difficult to read acronyms by eliminating the difference in the look of normal text and acronyms, for example, ASAP. They may also have unwanted effects on the reader.

For many years, the United States Weather Service used only capital letters in its bulletins, a practice dating to the time of teleprinter machines with only capital letters. This is how the weather service announced the change:

> April 11, 2016 LISTEN UP! BEGINNING ON MAY 11, NOAA'S NATIONAL WEATHER SERVICE FORECASTS WILL STOP YELLING AT YOU.[46]

Art Thomas, the weather service meteorologist in charge of the project, said, "We hope that using all caps for emphasis will get people's attention when it matters and encourage people to take action to protect their safety. We realized we could still use ALL CAPS within products to add emphasis, such as 'TORNADO WARNING. TAKE COVER NOW!'"[47]

Beyond Text

Pictures increase attention; they wake up and invigorate a listener's brain by shifting the mode of sensory input from audio to visual. They help a point come alive in the listener's mind and communicate subtleties difficult to put into words. They are a great way to create an emotional response and reinforce a point in a new way. (Remember: Two keys to creating a long-term memory are to evoke emotion and to leverage the listener's familiarity with a point or topic.) For visual learners, pictures can be the most powerful and effective part of your presentation.

Photographs

Photographs are the most popular images used on presentation slides. They give you options, precision, and subtlety. Photos, especially those of people, can evoke strong emotional responses. Audience members process photos quickly, using more emotion and less logic, than when processing text or spoken words. Keep this in mind if using a photo in an emotionally charged environment.

Nobody has ever taken a photograph of something they want to forget.
REBECCA MCNUTT

You can take a digital photo yourself, find one on the Web, purchase a stock photo, or import one from one of the many software packages that provide them. Search the internet under "stock photos" for a wide variety of resources. Even a familiar photo used in an unexpected way can be a great method of introducing a new idea or adding humor. With current topics, avoid dated-looking photos and images.

Image Size Should Equal or Exceed Screen Resolutions

When choosing images for PowerPoint or Keynote slides, pixels matter. DPI (dots per square inch) does not.

Start with screen resolution. The most common screen resolution as of early 2016 (expressed in pixels, width by length) was 1920 x 1080 for desktops and 1366 x 768 for laptops. But they differ, and screen resolutions continue to increase. You can find your screen resolution in the system preferences for your computer. You also have the option of changing the screen resolution on most computers, so you may want to choose one to work better with your chosen images.

If your image will completely fill the slide, and hence the display screen, the image size, also in pixels, should be at least equal to the screen resolution. So, if your screen has the common resolution of 1920 by 1080, your image should also be at least 1920 by 1080. If the image occupies only half the width and half the height of the slide, it should be at least 1366 / 2 or 683 pixels wide, and 768 / 2 or 384 pixels high.

To ensure clarity of highly detailed images you may choose images of a slightly higher resolution. You can experiment with different resolutions to find your best choice. Just keep in mind that the higher the resolution, the larger the file. Files that are too large may load more slowly. Choose a size that looks clear, but don't greatly exceed it.

Cropping

Crop out the unnecessary parts of an image to help focus on what matters. Check the size of the image before setting the cropping distances from each edge so that you can crop out just the right amount.

Brightness

Check before the presentation if possible; adjust the brightness as you finalize your presentation slides.

Graphics

Charts and graphs can help you present data so members of your audience can understand and interpret it more easily. Studies have shown that both understanding and retention go up when more than one sense is used to receive a message. Graphics also help hold listeners' attention by creating a change of pace.[48]

Business software packages have built-in graph creation tools that meet the needs of most presenters most of the time. You can find examples of charts, advice on the best kind of chart to use to present your data, and examples to look at in your presentation software, word processing software, and spreadsheet software.

Many different kinds of charts and graphs are used in specific fields. Specialized graphing software programs are available for technical and scientific specialties.

You can use built-in graphing tools to create a basic graph and then add other visual elements, such as lines, text boxes, or arrows. Another option is to import a graph from another software package.

Title

The graph's title should help the audience understand the point. "Sales Up 30 Percent Year-to-Date" is a stronger title than "Year-to-Date Sales Results."

Axes

Set the scales of the axes to be appropriate to the data being shown. Also, make sure that axis labels indicating the values along each axis are big enough to read easily.

Colors

The background color and the color of each data block or line should be high contrast and consistent with the overall color scheme of the slides. Consider any symbolic meaning of colors. Red may mean "in the red" for financial services audiences.

Depth

Three-dimensional images work best with bar, column, and pie graphs. Three-dimensional data blocks look solid and tangible. Find 3-D graphs among the choices of standard graphs in basic software packages.

Labels

Data labels add emphasis or precision to the values on a graph. Labels work best at the end of bars or columns, above data points on a line graph, or outside the sections in a pie graph. Place them close to the data point. Check that text is large enough, with enough color contrast. Keep labels consistent in style.

Legends

Use a legend when you have more than one element on a graph. The legend connects a data element to a color on the graph and makes the graph easier to understand.

Tombstones

A "tombstone" is a summary statement (what the audience should remember when this slide is "dead and gone") at the bottom of your slide. The tombstone can reinforce the title or further explain the data. For example, with the title "Sales Up 30 Percent Year-to-Date," the tombstone might be "Every region contributed to increase."

Tables

Tables are sets of columns and rows that hold and organize data without interpreting it. Tables are useful for raw data and allow the audience freedom of interpretation. You may want to include a table to show the thoroughness of your research and the richness of the data, and then use a graph to interpret the data for the audience.

Tables can be hard to read, so keep them to a reasonable size. No more than six rows and six columns is a good rule of thumb, and consider the audience's ability to see the screen. If you choose to interpret the data in a table without adding a graph, highlight or change the background color of the important cells, change the text color, make it bold, or both. Bold text on your column and row headings helps the audience read the table and find pertinent data more easily.

Presentation software packages have built-in table creation tools, and tables can be imported from other software packages as well. When you import, always test your slides on the same presentation equipment you will use for your presentation to make sure the imported table translated accurately.

Don't Oversimplify

Traffic signs have enough information to guide drivers and absolutely nothing more—nothing to distract them. They usually have just two high-contrast colors: white letters on deep green, black letters on goldenrod, white letters on red. They have large letters; clean, spare fonts; one or two words. An extremely simple graphic might be used: a round-headed stick figure walking, two bold lines merging, two bold lines crossed. Their simple, distinctive shapes—triangles, octagons, and rectangles—are easy to recognize and understand.

Billboards also communicate just one idea, with one large picture, just a few words with huge letters. Is a traffic sign or a billboard a good model for an ideal slide?

Everything should be made as simple as possible. But not simpler.

ALBERT EINSTEIN

No. Here's why. Very few ideas you talk about will be as simple or familiar to your audience as the messages on traffic signs and billboards. Simple traffic signs and billboards remind people of concepts they already know, especially when they are driving by. They are not a good way to communicate new material, more complex information, or the differences between two or more things. A "traffic sign" approach to slide design won't help your listeners see an emerging trend. It won't give them the subtle details that will help them make a fully informed decision. It won't help them choose between two emotionally charged options. A visual aid that helps listeners understand and remember important information demands and deserves more conscious attention than a traffic sign.

Yale professor and guru of visual presentation of information Edward Tufte is a severe critic of the oversimplified design of many electronic slides. Tufte points to oversimplification as a major cause of the slide overdose that far too many presenters try to pour down the throats of listeners. This oversimplification, Tufte believes, is encouraged by electronic slide software, specifically PowerPoint. Tufte explains that the typical PowerPoint slide shows about forty words and can be read in about eight seconds, and states, "With so little information per slide, many, many slides are needed. Audiences consequently endure a relentless sequentiality, one damn slide after another."[49]

Tufte believes strongly that complexity, detail, and the showing of information side by side—not in sequence—are often needed to achieve understanding. Especially when presenting statistical data and complex technical information, more detail often means greater clarity and understanding. The side-by-side presentation of information is what makes it possible to explain relationships, compare and contrast, and assign value.

When people look at my pictures I want them to feel the way they do when they want to read a line of a poem twice.

ROBERT FRANK

This makes sense. But it also raises a question. Why do the presentation software templates (and most presentation training guides) recommend slides that are so simple? I think this is a well-intentioned response to too much unnecessary detail. Too many presenters use slides that are so complicated, filled with so much text and so many graphics, they become not just hard to understand but often hard to see or read.

The Right Visual Balance

Slides demand the right balance between the needed detail and the clearest possible design. Both text and graphics must be large enough so your listeners see them clearly.

Presentation software has many features that can be used to create slides that are as simple or as detailed as you need. These features give you control and flexibility to go beyond the standard templates. Many fields—finance, technology, mathematics, and the different branches of science—have other software specifically designed to help communicate specialized and complex information effectively.

The Advantages of Detailed Slides

More detail on slides makes it necessary to move more slowly through these slides. Moving more slowly gives listeners a chance to understand and digest the more complex information. Aim to combine more detailed slides and a slower pace with intermittent use of simpler slides or no slides at all. This creates changes in pace that keep your audience more attentive. But do not deliberately create complicated or detailed slides. Don't worry if you include details or complexity that is essential to your message. Include detail if it is germane. Just make sure your listeners can see it.

The Law of Visual Aid Supply and Demand

The Law of Visual Aid Supply and Demand states, "Every added visual aid reduces the importance of the others."

Too many slides insult the listeners' intelligence, and then they bore, numb, and lull. Sometimes a single detailed slide is needed, not twelve simpler ones. Part of the solution is to recognize that slides are not your speaker notes. Speak without slides part of the time. Create pictures in the minds of listeners in other ways: use an analogy, tell a story, describe something using gestures, or have the listeners close their eyes and picture it.

Have Outside Eyes Triple Check Your Slides

Have someone who did not create the slides check the final product. Because our brains fill in pieces to create a recognizable picture, you are too likely to see what you meant to say at the expense of the actual text, spelling, visibility, and overall effectiveness of the slide. It is vital to have a third party check your slides for accuracy. This is easy to do, and not doing it may be costly.

When Nike wooed Stephen Curry, the National Basketball Association's Most Valuable Player Award Winner, as a spokesperson, several things went wrong, but a mistake on a slide sealed the coffin.

According to Dell Curry—a sports commentator, retired NBA player, and Stephen Curry's father and advisor—the meeting began badly when a Nike executive mispronounced Stephen's name. "I heard some people pronounce his name wrong before," said Dell Curry. "I wasn't surprised. I was surprised that I didn't get a correction." Later, a slide with Kevin Durant's name, probably recycled from a pitch meant for Durant, came up. "I stopped paying attention after that," Dell Curry said. A short time later, Stephen Curry signed a contract to be a spokesperson for Under Armour.[50]

Summary

A visual aid should be visual. It should aid your listeners in understanding and remembering your information. The best visual aids are germane to your content, that is, they cannot be removed without harming understanding.

Choose the best visual aids for your message, your audience, and your speaking venue. Choose visual elements—charts, graphs, and photos—carefully. Many different software programs exist for creating charts and graphs. Word processing, spreadsheet, and presentation software all have examples and guidelines to follow when creating visual aids. More specialized software for disciplines such as science, mathematics, and medicine is available as well.

Colors of the background, text, and visual images should be chosen with your audience in mind. Consider both legibility and aesthetic appeal when choosing a text style and size: Generally, the simpler and bigger, the better.

8

Never wear anything that panics the cat.

P. J. O'ROURKE

YOU LOOK MARVELOUS!

What to Wear, Where

You are your first visual aid.

Your appearance will speak before you do. It is an important part of the first impression you create, an impression that will either support or detract from your ability to influence your audience. Whether or not you believe your audience *should* judge you on your appearance, they will. Understand this, and dress and groom yourself in ways that will support your message.

Business attire is much more varied than it was in years past. Different organizations, industries, and geographic regions all can have different dress codes. Now more than ever, your choice of what to wear is influenced by the type of presentation, your knowledge of your audience and their expectations, and the venue or setting.

Be Clear About Your Goal

Are you coming to represent *your* position, company, or industry, or are you coming to fit in with *theirs?*

If you are approaching another company's management team about a joint venture, dressing as they do can help create a feeling of shared identity. If you want to establish your credentials as a banker, you need to dress for the expectations your audience will have for a banker. If you develop software, the expectations will be different. If you are a creative artist, they will be different again.

If you are an interior designer presenting your ideas for a new boutique hotel, your personal ensemble can show you understand how well-chosen colors, textures, and accessories create a special look. If you come to seek funds to continue excavating a Wari village in the Andes of Peru, wearing the latest Italian silk suit will probably raise some questions about where the funds are going. But ripped and dirty field clothes will not show respect for the audience and occasion.

Some reasonable compromise between highly formal and extremely casual is usually needed. If you aren't sure about the right choice, or if you just aren't that interested in fashion, get some advice from someone you respect. Many companies offer the services of fashion consultants who can assess your looks, help you update them, and work with you to put together a wardrobe that can serve you well.

I am Professor Feynman, in spite of the suit-coat. I usually give lectures in shirtsleeves but when I started out of the hotel this morning my wife said "You must wear a suit." I said "But I usually give lectures in shirtsleeves." She said "Yes, but this time you don't know what you're talking about so you had better make a good impression…" So, I got a coat.

RICHARD FEYNMAN

Choose what is appropriate for the occasion.

Everyone has many choices in today's world. If you are unsure of how formally you should dress, ask the organizers of the event. If you are still unsure, dress more formally rather than less to demonstrate respect for the occasion and the audience. This also helps give you credibility and an air of authority without appearing out of place.

Business Casual

Clean, well-pressed, and well-fitted clothes are a must. Avoid extremes of color or style. Choose clothing that is simple and well fitted, comfortable, and not too revealing. A jackets, sweater, or scarf makes it possible to add or remove a layer to suit the temperature of the venue.

Choose shoes you can walk in easily and comfortably. Avoid sandals, open-toed shoes, and athletic shoes unless you are speaking poolside or courtside. Accessories should remain reasonably conservative and limited to avoid becoming distracting. Costume jewelry may be appropriate but should still be minimal and of good quality.

Personal Grooming for Business

Hair

Hair should be clean and styled in a conservative and flattering manner. If you have had the same hairstyle for several years, get an honest and objective opinion about it. If you decide to make a change, invest in a good cut. And do so a week before your presentation. This will give you time to get used to the new you.

Don't let your hair cover your eyebrows or hang in your face. People need to see your eyes and your facial expressions. Continually brushing or tossing aside your hair is extremely distracting so choose an appropriate style and use hair spray if needed. Beards and mustaches should be neatly trimmed and should not cover your lips. Age-related hair growth, e.g., visible hair in and around the ears and nose, should be removed. Eyebrows should be shaped and trimmed as needed.

Makeup

Makeup should enhance your look, not hide you or recreate you. Makeovers are available at the cosmetic counters in reputable department and specialty stores and are a good way to learn how to update your look. Explain your purpose to the makeup artist, or choose an artist with a look you find appropriate.

Generally, stay with more subtle colors that work well with both your skin tone and the outfit you plan to wear. If you tend to perspire, avoid makeup that can melt and run. Powder can help prevent shine. If speaking under bright lights, more makeup may be appropriate as bright lights can wash out your natural color. If you will speak on television, ask if a makeup artist will be provided, and how much time you should allow for your makeup session.

Hands and Nails

Your hands should be clean and your nails manicured. If you polish your nails, choose an appropriate color. Avoid extreme differences in the length of your nails.

Last Look

Just before your presentation, ask someone to give you a quick once-over just to make sure that buttons are buttoned, zippers are zipped, and static electricity hasn't left one trouser leg attached to your shin.

Clothes make the man. Naked people have little or no influence in society.
MARK TWAIN

Summary

Whether or not they should be, your dress and overall appearance are important sources of nonverbal information. Your listeners will make quick and often subconscious judgments about you based on the visual clues you give. If the initial judgments are positive, you will find a more receptive audience. A negative first impression can be very hard—even impossible—to overcome.

Choose clothing based on your goals. To emphasize similarities between you and your listeners, you may want to dress as they do. If you want to be seen as an expert, wear more formal dress or clothing that identifies you as an expert in your field. If you are in doubt about what is appropriate, ask ahead of time. If still in doubt, dress more formally rather than less. Conservative choices that do not distract the audience from your message are generally best. Neatness and cleanliness are a must. Your clothes should be clean, well fitted, and in good condition. Your skin, hair, and nails should also be clean and well cared for. Your appearance should show self-respect as well as respect of your listeners and of the occasion.

PART III

DELIVER A POLISHED PRESENTATION

9

I'm in the back of a limousine with Charlie Chaplin
and it's 1928. Charlie is beautiful;
his body language seems to skip, and reel and rhyme,
heartbreaking and witty at the same time.
It seems to promise a better world.

GEOFF RYMAN

YOUR BODY SPEAKS

The Power of Your Body Language

Reading Your Listeners' Body Language

Before we consider how your listeners will use your body language to interpret your meaning, let's consider what we already know. Reading body language helps you evaluate whether you are communicating well. Table 9.1 lists some common components of body language and their likely meanings. It can be used to raise your awareness of your listeners' needs during your presentation. You may be surprised at what you already know. The key is putting this knowledge to work.

Table 9.1 Interpreting Body Language

This body language	*May mean this:*
Nodding head	Understanding, agreement, approval
Shaking head	Disagreement, dissension, disapproval
Head cocked to one side	Thinking, considering, skepticism
Narrowed eyes, furrowed brow	Thinking, analysis, evaluation
Rolling eyes	That is obvious, impractical, stupid
Rubbing of eyes	Doubt, disbelief, tiredness, suspicion
Coughing	Nervousness, preparation to speak
Deep sighing	Boredom, impatience, disinterest
Light sighing	Thoughtfulness, interest
Hands in front of mouth	Embarrassment, reluctance to speak
Smiling	Confidence, enjoyment, politeness
Smirking	Smugness, condescension
Leaning back, slumping, turning	Disinterest, detachment
Hands open with palms up	Sincerity
Counting points on fingers	Organization, logic, confidence
Steepling of fingers	Self-confidence, strength
Pointing	Singling out, aggressiveness
Wagging finger	Pedantry, warning, disagreement
Arms crossed in front of chest	Judgment, resistance, defensiveness
Hands below chest, palms up	Helplessness, plea for help or consideration
Hands in pockets	Relaxation, reservation, little involvement
One hand above head	Emphasis, differentiation
Two hands above head	Success, triumph

So, you already know a great deal about body language. Just a look at Table 9.1 shows how much we know—possibly much more than we realized. Watch your listeners. Good eye contact makes a lot of watching possible. Learn from their body language to tailor your material. You can recognize when you need to clarify, explain, expound, give an example, offer to stop and answer questions, and adjust your pace as needed. Remember that body language is always open to interpretation. Individual habits, cultural differences, even the temperature in the room can all affect body language. Crossed arms may mean a listener is chilled, not defensive. Be flexible in your interpretations of the body language of others.

> You can do a lot of observing just by watching.
> YOGI BERRA

Your listeners are just as savvy, just as skilled. Whether your listeners are watching you or you are watching them, body language is a big part of the message. Your true feelings will "leak" into your message through your body language. With that in mind, let's look at some specifics to using body language to polish your presentation.

Using Body Language

Nonverbal messages are an important part of a polished presentation, but we often don't give our own body language much attention. Yet these messages supplement, reinforce, emphasize, soften, and add subtle but powerful shades of meaning to our communications.

We use them every time we speak. Our dialogues are rich with them and richer because of them. We need to use these nonverbal means of communication to deliver a complete presentation. They matter. But while we have a great deal of formal training in the complexities of spoken and written language, we usually have little conscious awareness of our own body language. Yet body language will change, supplement, support, or contradict the words we use.

The normal challenges and stresses of speaking to a group affect your ability to use these delivery skills naturally and effectively. When you become the salient object, things feel different. You become self-conscious, hyperaware of your body. The fight-or-flight response battles with the knowledge that you must stay where you are and speak—and deliver a monologue. The body reacts instinctively. It searches for ways to feel more comfortable. You may stiffen or shift your weight. You may put your hands in your pockets and keep them there or hold them together in front of your stomach for many minutes at a time in an instinctive move to protect your vital organs. Your eyes may look away from your listeners or move so quickly that you never focus on anyone, an instinctive response that eliminates the direct look that can escalate into a confrontation. Awareness of how your body responds to this self-consciousness is the first step to returning to more natural, conversational uses of body language. Practice and feedback—video feedback is by far the best—are both needed to become truly skillful in delivering your message well.

Consistency between the verbal and nonverbal parts of your message is the key to looking natural, comfortable, and confident. It is an important part of establishing credibility in the minds of listeners. This is especially true when you are speaking to people who don't already know you well. The bottom line is this: To be most effective, *how* you say something needs to be consistent with *what* you say.

Learning to use nonverbal communication well won't require building new muscles or stretching them in new ways. You will simply be reminding your body of what it does when you aren't self-conscious. Because the skills aren't new, it doesn't take years to master them. It just takes consciousness, reminders, and practice. When you start to use more of your everyday nonverbal communication habits when speaking to a group, you will speak in a natural, confident, and comfortable way.

> **Language is a more recent technology. Your body language, your eyes, your energy will come through to your audience before you even start speaking.**
>
> PETER GUBER

How Important Is Good Nonverbal Communication?

Good content is not a substitute for good nonverbal communication. If body language undermines your verbal message, you will not succeed in winning over the minds and hearts of your listeners. You need to "say it like you mean it." Understanding and using the nonverbal delivery skills described on the following pages will help you look and sound more natural, confident, and comfortable.

Good Nonverbal Delivery Skills Dampen Anxiety

The subtitle of this chapter is The Power of Your Body Language. *Your* is there for a reason. You use a unique combination of nonverbal behaviors. Your goal is to hold onto them when speaking to a group. This isn't always easy. Yet, your awareness of what you do, and how and when you do it when relaxed, is the key to using nonverbal behaviors in your presentation.

When you think other people notice your anxiety, you become even more anxious. You sense that listeners will question your knowledge, ability, or conviction if they notice signs of anxiety. That anxiety causes more anxiety. Anxiety makes us stiffen, abandon much of the natural body language we use so effectively, and, sometimes, start doing other things we wouldn't normally do.

Good nonverbal delivery skills make it impossible to tell that you don't feel as comfortable and as confident as you look and sound. Any remaining anxiety is invisible to listeners. When you know that others cannot see or hear your anxiety, you relax. As you master the use of these skills, you will be able to focus more easily on what you want to say and how best to say it.

These changes won't take place overnight. Your body, drawing on all its Stone Age wisdom, will protest when you ask it to stop protecting your vital organs by clasping both hands in front of you. It will protest when you ask it to stand balanced and tall instead of shifting back and forth. It will even protest when you ask it to finish a point, stop, and take a deep breath: "I'm standing here totally exposed, greatly outnumbered, and you want me to *relax*? Are you *crazy*?"

Some very experienced speakers have very poor delivery skills and engrained nervous habits that may have made the speakers feel more comfortable when they started making presentations and then became habits. That doesn't mean they work well. But who's going to be the one to tell the CEO that they annoy everyone when they stand onstage constantly "washing" their hands?

Practice, coaching, and video feedback are the fastest ways to integrate good nonverbal delivery skills with your spoken content. Even if you've been making presentations for years, you should take a fresh look at yourself. With the technology available today, this is easy to do.

Steel and Sparks

The two types of nonverbal delivery skills are "steel" skills and "spark" skills. Using both is the secret to looking—and becoming—comfortable and confident.

Steel Skills:

These skills communicate strength, confidence, and honesty. The three steel skills are eye contact, pace (including the pause), and posture. You will use them to communicate with authority and composure.

Eye Contact

What are your immediate responses to these phrases?

- A steady gaze
- They looked each other in the eyes

And to these?

- They looked down at their feet
- Shifty eyes

Steady eye contact is a powerful way to communicate confidence and honesty. Let's look at how we use eye contact when engaged in unself-conscious dialogue.

In one-on-one conversations and when speaking in very small groups, most people look each other in the eye. The speaker shows a desire to "connect with" the listener, and observes the listener's reaction—does the listener understand, show confusion or concern, agree or disagree?

Yet eyes that shift too quickly are the norm for unskilled speakers. And then comes the bad advice: "Look at the back wall. Look at their foreheads. Pretend they are in their underwear. Imagine them naked." Seriously? These behaviors do not help. To establish and maintain effective eye contact, try these recommended actions.

- *Begin and end your presentation by sweeping the audience with your eyes.* This honors your natural tendency to check the situation over and gather people together.

- *During the rest of the presentation, look at one person in the eyes while you deliver a point, a phrase, or sentence.* As in dialogue, aim for approximately three to six seconds of steady eye contact before moving on. You communicate confidence, honesty, interest in your audience, but not aggression. You can watch for listeners' reactions, read your audience, and respond.

- *Look at people in all parts of the audience without a recognizable sequence.* Look at individuals in front, back, sides, and the third balcony. All the listeners will feel more involved and valued, and so will be more attentive.

- *Avoid spending a disproportionate amount of time on "decision makers."* You will avoid being perceived as giving someone preferential treatment. You will involve everyone, including those who may have influence in events to come.

- *Look at people when speaking.* If you need to break eye contact to think or to check your notes or visual aids, pause and breathe while doing so. You avoid "data dump" and increase appropriate pauses.

- *Learn about and honor individual or cultural preferences for lengths of eye contact.* You establish rapport and respect and avoid appearing evasive, insensitive, or overbearing.

Pace and Pause

Our natural speech patterns are musical. Variations in tempo, pace, and the frequency and length of the pauses—the "rests"—communicate varying degrees of emphasis and a wide range of emotions. Some of us speak more quickly, some at a slower, more measured pace. Our speech reflects our own thinking styles and cultural differences as well as the nature of our content, but we all vary our pace, our tone, and the frequency and length of our pauses.

Pauses punctuate speech. Pauses are the commas, periods, colons, and semicolons of speech. They are indentations at the beginning of new paragraphs and white space at the end of a chapter. We wouldn't write a memo, much less a story, without using punctuation.

> The notes I handle no better than many pianists. But the pauses between the notes— ah, that is where the art resides.
> ARTUR SCHNABEL

The challenges of speaking before a group can combine to rob us of the natural timing we use so skillfully in dialogue. The release of adrenaline may make us speak more rapidly. But listeners need time to process information, to think about what it means to them, to experience the emotional response your information brings—to feel the excitement, enthusiasm, concern.

To keep your great natural timing, try the tips that follow.

- *Slow down.* You will sound more natural and genuine. Your listeners can process and appreciate your information. Remember, it is not what you give them that matters; it is what they get.

- *Punctuate your speech with pauses.* They add meaning, emphasis, and interest.

> He had occasional flashes of silence that made his conversation perfectly delightful.
> SYDNEY SMITH

- *Breathe deeply when you pause.* You need oxygen. It is easier to relax and avoid extraneous filler words. Use diaphragmatic breathing, breathing more slowly and deeply than you may tend to do when anxious. This will expend less effort and energy to breathe, and can reduce many of the physical symptoms of anxiety.

- *Pause and breathe when you change slides and check notes.* You will look—and be—more confident, relaxed, and in control.

Posture

Your listeners will assess your confidence before you begin to speak. When they first see you, the way you hold your body suggests how you feel about yourself and your information. Good posture doesn't take years of practice. You can do it right now and use it throughout your presentations.

When walking to the front of the room or on stage, keep your head up and your shoulders back. If seated where listeners see you before you begin to speak, whether in a chair onstage or behind a table as a panelist, you are already communicating to them. When seated, sit upright and rest your hands in your lap or, if seated at one, on top of the table.

A relaxed, confident posture helps reduce the symptoms of the fight-or-flight response. Good posture increases confidence and the ability to relax. It opens your chest and lungs to allow you to breathe deeply and give your body and brain the oxygen they need to help you perform at your best.

To maintain good posture and communicate confidence, energy, openness, use these tips.

- *Balance your weight evenly with your feet several inches apart.* This stance communicates confidence, energy, and shows you are comfortable being the center of attention.

- *Stand tall.* Hold your head high, your shoulders back. You take full advantage of your height, increasing your personal presence. You appear confident and energetic. This posture opens your diaphragm for easy breathing.

- *Stand firmly.* Avoid shifting or rocking back and forth. You look both confident and relaxed. You will find more effective ways (gestures, movement) to dissipate your natural energy.

- *Stand facing the entire audience.* No matter where you are on the speaking platform, stop and stand with your toes and shoulders pointing to the center of the room. You can establish eye contact with any member of the audience, and all listeners will feel included.

- *Rest your arms at your sides when not gesturing.* Letting go of tension in your arms helps you look relaxed and non-defensive. Your arms and hands will now be free to use in natural and appropriate gestures.

It is no coincidence that mountain pose (tadasana) in yoga practice, so named because it evokes the power of a mountain—the height, strength, and stability—looks very much like the posture described above. The ancient practice of yoga, developed to help us deal with the challenges we face in our daily lives, has stood the test of time. This posture helps you develop strength and a relaxed confidence, and makes it possible to breathe deeply and calmly. Good posture communicates this strength and confidence to your listeners. Step-by-step instructions for mountain pose, similar to the steps that follow, are spoken every day by yoga instructors all over the world.

1. Stand with your feet parallel beneath your hips, about the width of two fists between your feet.

2. Lift up and spread all your toes; balance your weight evenly on the balls and heels of your feet. Keeping your toes spread, set them down.

3. Add (and maintain) a "micro-bend" to your knees, bringing your shins slightly forward. Avoid locking your knees.

4. Engage the quadriceps and draw them upward.

5. Rotate both thighs slightly inward, widening the pelvis.

6. Maintain the natural curves of your spine. Add a slight tuck of the tailbone, drawing it down toward your feet.

7. Engage the belly, drawing your navel toward your spine.

8. Lift your chest, widen your collarbones, and make sure your shoulders are directly over your hips.

9. Roll your shoulders up and back, releasing your shoulder blades down your back.

10. Let the crown of your head rise so your neck is long and your chin is parallel to the ground.

11. Let your arms hang naturally with the elbows slightly bent and thumbs rotated slightly out.

12. Smile and breathe!

To check your alignment yourself, stand in mountain pose with your back against the wall. The backs of your heels, tailbone, and shoulder blades should touch the wall, with the back of your head just slightly forward from the wall. An observer can tell you are aligned well when the centers of your ear, shoulder joint, outer hip, and anklebone are in one line, perpendicular to the floor.

Develop the habit of standing this way to prevent slouching, rocking from hip to hip, or stepping nervously in a small space. This balanced posture also communicates a relaxed alertness, and allows spontaneous and purposeful movement in any direction with no sense of awkwardness.

Spark Skills

Spark skills add energy, enthusiasm, and variety to your style. The four spark skills are facial expressions, voice, gestures, and movement (including the use of space). Use of spark skills can vary greatly with the nature of your content. Master the spark skills to keep the audience attentive and engaged.

Facial Expressions

Facial expressions can transcend cultural norms and cultural differences. Infants respond to facial expressions long before they understand the meaning of words. Throughout life humans continue to "speak" with and "listen" to facial expressions when communicating with words and sentences.

Some people become quite skilled at not using facial expressions—cultivating the ability to maintain a poker face or display only those emotions they believe are socially acceptable. They hide their feelings behind a mask of "professionalism." Over time, this can reduce the natural tendency for our facial expressions to support our spoken messages.

Self-consciousness, intense concentration on content, and fear may reduce your natural tendency to use facial expressions freely. If so, you often won't look as if you mean what you say. This inconsistency between verbal and nonverbal messages can be disconcerting to your listeners. It interferes with your ability to communicate confidence, honesty, enthusiasm—or any other emotion supporting your message. It can strongly affect your listeners' assessment of you and your material.

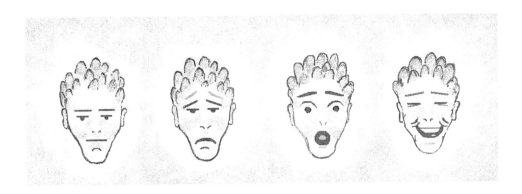

Awareness of the importance of facial expressions, and of your own individual, natural facial expressions, will help you use them to create the look and feel of dialogue. Here are tips for using facial expressions well.

- *Use a variety of appropriate facial expressions throughout your presentation.* Your expressions will support your content, and you will communicate confidence and honesty.

- *At times, show your emotion rather than telling it.* A warm smile does a better job of saying "I'm delighted to be here" than the words do without the smile. You will encourage people to look at you and increase their ability to stay focused. This will evoke more emotional responses and improve your listeners' ability to remember.

- *Smile frequently, unless the mood is sober or somber.* Anxiety makes us smile less frequently than we otherwise might. A smile communicates warmth, good humor, and relaxation. It is contagious, improving the mood and receptivity of your listeners.

- *Observe the variety and power of facial expressions used by others.* You will develop a better understanding of how much is enough and how much is too much and will feel more comfortable

- *Watch television and videos with the sound off.* Describe the emotions shown, even in silence. Then recreate the expressions looking in a mirror. You will increase your understanding of how even subtle changes in expression affect the message.

Voice

Variety is the key to a natural and conversational voice. Variations in tone, pitch, pace, and volume create the sound and feeling of dialogue. Tone is vital; changes in tone can completely change the meaning of words.

Video with sound captures the relationship between your voice, your face, and your body language. Record yourself at some length; you will get more and better insight than you can just listening to your phone greeting or a voice message.

Your recorded voice will sound different than it sounds to you when you speak. We hear through our bones, not just our ears, and bones are a good conductor of sound. Added to and blended with what we hear through our ears, the voice we hear through the bones of our body is different from what others hear. A recording device picks up only the sounds that travel through the air and, even electronically reproduced, gives us a sound closer to what others hear. Listen closely for pitch, tone, modulation, and rate of speech. Work on any issues you find by repeating, and recording, the same sentence until you achieve the desired result.

> His voice is deep and gravelly. I once heard one of the girls say that he had the voice of a sex god, but because I've never really heard what a sex god sounds like, I can't verify that.
>
> MELINA MARCHETTA

Deep, rich voices are pleasing, but a monotonous deep voice is deadly. Our natural dialogue tends to be greatly varied in modulation, pitch, and even the rate of speech. Research has shown that when we speak louder, as we do when trying to be heard over a din, we also tend to speak with purer, more musical tones. This happens regardless of musical ability or training. Researchers believe it may be caused by unconsciously trying to capitalize on the emotional qualities of music to capture our listeners' attention.[51] Confidence in your material is no guarantee of a voice that communicates with confidence and energy. Get to know your voice, and practice making any changes you know will improve it.

The voice is a wind instrument. Frequent and deep breathing supply air. This means breathing deeply while you pause to replenish the air supply. To add variety to your voice, try the tips that follow.

- *Speak loudly enough to be heard easily by everyone in the audience.* If in doubt, ask for feedback on your volume.

- *If you need a microphone, use one.* Speak naturally, without strain, without shouting, without excess drama. Do not adopt the style of speakers from the time before microphones who had to do these things to be heard. You don't. Continuing these behaviors makes you seem to be performing, not sharing.

- *Use a cordless, small, clip-on microphone when possible.* It frees your hands, frees you to move, and eliminates the danger of tripping on a cord.

- *Vary your volume.* You make it easier for listeners to pay attention.

- *Increase your volume at times.* You will communicate importance, urgency, and confidence.

- *Decrease your volume to create a feeling of intimacy.* People may listen more closely.

- *Vary your tone.* Your voice will support your content and emotion.

- *Use higher tones at times.* Higher tones communicate excitement, enthusiasm, and energy.

- *Use lower tones at times.* Lower tones communicate gravity and conviction.

- *Breathe deeply before you speak and when you pause.* You will have the air you need to think and project with natural tones, and breathing helps you relax.

Gestures

"What should I do with my hands?"

You should do exactly what you do (with a few obvious exceptions) when speaking one-on-one or in a small group.

We use gestures naturally and unself-consciously during dialogue. We use them without much conscious awareness. The heightened self-awareness during a presentation makes us more aware of our hands and we may second-guess our gestures and wonder if they are appropriate.

The sense of vulnerability during a presentation can lead to overly self-protective gestures. Most inexperienced speakers will clasp their hands in front of their chest, stomach, or groin. It's no coincidence that their hands end up in front of their "soft underbelly," protecting vital organs. This served our ancestors as protection against threats but doesn't help us to relax, look confident, or use gestures to help us communicate.

For most of us, the more subtle a gesture is the more persuasive it is.

ANNETTE SIMMONS

Gestures have purpose. They illustrate, emphasize, and punctuate our speech. Author and storyteller Annette Simmons explains, "Gestures can add meaning to your story, intensify your message, and create a stage upon which your story is played… to increase the intensity of emotion, to intentionally send an incongruent message, or just to have a bit of fun."

Types of Gestures

We do a lot with gestures, one more excellent reason not to keep your hands in your pockets or clasped behind your back. Consider these different types and what they add to language.

- *Symbolic*. Have you ever nodded your head to say yes or shaken it to say no? Have you ever held up your hand, palm out and fingers pointing up, to signal someone to stop? If so, you've used what researchers call symbolic gestures.

- *Indicative*. Have you ever pointed a finger to show someone that something is "over there," or "that way"? If so, you've used indicative gestures.

- *Motor*. Have you ever noticed yourself "chopping" the air, holding your hand in a fairly rigid position as you move it up and down? This is a motor gesture. Motor gestures are usually repeated several times, emphasizing a point.

- *Lexical*. Studies have shown that when speakers are prevented from using their hands, they take longer to access words or even fail to come up with them at all. Drawing small circles in the air when you have trouble finding the right word can help you access your vocabulary, or lexicon. This is a lexical gesture.[52]

Most of us have little awareness of our own repertoire of gestures and can be uncomfortable gesturing in front of a group. To increase your comfort, increase your awareness of your habits.

- *Observe your gestures as you talk to become aware of your own gestural habits and repertoire.* You will be more comfortable in front of a group when your gestures are familiar.

- *Observe the gestures others use.* You will learn what works well and expand your repertoire.

- *Use a variety of gestures.* Avoid frequent, repetitive gestures of just the hands and wrists. You will avoid looking mechanical, stiff, or overly repetitive.

- *Use subtle head and upper body gestures.* You will be more natural and therefore more believable and persuasive.

- *Use expansive gestures at times.* Gestures of the whole arm and body look confident and energetic and help project your voice.

- *Illustrate objects, images, and concepts and actions with gestures.* This helps your audience visualize and understand your material. It can also jumpstart your use of other natural gestures.

- *Drop your arms to rest at your sides when not gesturing.* You look relaxed and open, and avoid nervous hand clasping, handwringing, or other distracting habits. Now your hands are available to gesture again.

Movement

How long can someone look at a statue? Not as long as you will speak. Movement commands attention and communicates confidence. Natural and purposeful, energetic movement in the space you are given is an important skill to master.

Things in motion sooner catch the eye than what not stirs.
WILLIAM SHAKESPEARE

Standing still, especially if you're partially hidden by a lectern or table, increases the feeling of separation and reduces similarity between the monologue you present and the dialogue of daily speech. Movement allows you to minimize the distance between you and members of the audience. It demonstrates comfort with your environment and gives sense of ownership and command of your material and the occasion.

Movement does not mean pacing. But like pacing, it helps you relax, burn off adrenaline-induced energy, and think more clearly.

Movement is not a skill to use in front of a camera during an interview or video teleconference. Then your other skills must be tapped to communicate energy, confidence, and ownership. But, when possible and appropriate, arrange your venue so that you can move freely and safely.

Here are ways to use purposeful but intermittent movement to increase attention and communicate authority.

- *Use most of the space available.* This shows confidence and a sense of ownership of the occasion.

- *To move, establish eye contact with one person in the audience; move toward that person while speaking.* Now your movement has purpose: You are "bringing" the information to them. The continued individual eye contact keeps your movement focused and intentional.

- *Move intermittently to avoid pacing.* Punctuate your pacing movement with periods of balanced posture in one place to avoid the impression of nervous pacing and reap the benefits of increased audience attention.

- *Vary the direction, pace, and distance of your movement.* Match your movement to the nature and tone of your content. Your movement will support your message. You will move more naturally and avoid inconsistency between your spoken and visual messages.

- *Move at a natural pace.* Avoid slow, ponderous, or lethargic movement. Unnaturally slow movement looks self-conscious and tentative. A quicker, more natural pace is more confident.

- *Avoid overly aggressive or invasive movement.* Generally maintain at least four feet of "social" space between you and your listeners so they will feel involved, not threatened or singled out.

A blur of blinks, taps, jiggles, pivots and shifts…the body language of a man wishing urgently to be elsewhere.

EDWARD R. MURROW

Summary

Body language speaks before we say our first word, and nonverbal communication matters.

The fight-or-flight response, a natural reaction to the stress of public speaking, can cause us to behave in cautious and defensive ways, behaviors that increase our nervousness by interfering with our ability to release tension. They can also make us look and sound as if we are not confident or knowledgeable. Using the seven nonverbal delivery skills as we do when we are relaxed, unself-conscious, and confident is the key to great delivery.

Delivery skills can be divided into two groups. "Steel" skills communicate strength and confidence. "Spark" skills communicate emotion and energy.

The three steel skills are eye contact, pace/pause (the pace of speech and use of pauses), and posture. Steel skills are the solid foundation of your delivery style. They communicate strength, confidence, honesty, and composure. Master these steel skills to communicate with both calmness and authority.

Spark skills add energy, emotion, and variety to your style. The four spark skills are facial expressions, voice, gestures, and movement. The use of spark skills can vary greatly with the nature of your content, environment, and purpose. Master your spark skills to keep the audience attentive, engaged, and emotionally involved.

Watch your listeners to observe their body language. Be willing to tailor your presentation to meet their needs. Above all, remember you are at your best when you are uniquely you.

> We have to wake up. We have to refuse to be a clone.
>
> ALICE WALKER

10

Men have become the tools of their tools.

HENRY DAVID THOREAU

GIZMOS AND GADGETS

Using Tools of the Trade

Managed well, notes, visual aids, lecterns, microphones, and teleprompters can be enormously helpful for both speaker and audience. When managed poorly, they can ruin a presentation.

Tools add a layer of complexity to presentations. One challenge is maintaining good nonverbal delivery skills when using tools. A number of questions may come up:

- Can I use good eye contact when I use notes or slides?

- Can I keep the attention of the audience if I pause to change a slide?

- Can I create a sense of dialogue if I'm standing behind a lectern?

- Can I still move around the speaking platform with a microphone, notes, or slides?

The answer to all these questions is "Yes." With a little information and practice, you can do all these things. The information follows, and the practice is up to you.

Using Notes

You know it will be hard to remember what, when, and how to say everything you plan to present. Three common solutions are to create detailed slides to serve as speaker notes, write a script to read, or try to memorize the script. These approaches create new problems.

Putting all (or even most) of the information on slides almost always results in awful slides. They will be too complex for listeners to easily read, understand, or remember. Putting bullet point after bullet point on a slide may make a guide that is easy for you to follow, but don't kid yourself. This is not a visual aid. This is a sheet of speaker notes that you put on a screen. It is a script, in short form. It is a handout on a screen. But it is not a visual aid for listeners. It is an aid for the speaker.

> **Right now I'm having amnesia and déjà vu at the same time. I think I've forgotten this before.**
> STEVEN WRIGHT

Reading a script sounds stilted, fosters overdependence on the script, and makes it almost impossible to create rapport with the audience or make on-the-spot changes.

Memorizing the script and reciting it from memory has these problems and more. With memory unreliable under stress, the speaker is vulnerable to memory loss. Memorizing is also just plain inefficient. It's a terrible use of time.

The solution is to use notes with skill and without apologizing. You learned to develop the content of your presentation and to make notes in Chapter 3. You have notes, so use them.

Would you apologize for coming to a meeting with an agenda, for making a list to take grocery shopping, or for bringing a trail guide and a compass when hiking in the mountains? Of course not. Checking notes is not cheating. It shows you "plan your work and work your plan." It shows you want to give your audience full value. You can do all these things without staying behind a lectern. Here is a way to check notes worth practicing until you can do it with confidence and comfort.

Speak, Read, Speak

These three steps show confidence when you use notes.

1. Leave the lectern and walk to the front and center of the speaking area or platform. Cover a point or two. When you are close to finishing a point and need to check your notes, finish the point you are on with a confident tone and demeanor.

2. Do not start the next sentence. Instead, pause to let the audience think about the completed point. Turn, walk briskly to the lectern, and face your notes straight

on (rather than leaning toward them from a distance or looking at them over your shoulder while your body faces the audience).

3. Read until you have all the information you need. Really read—do not rush. The more deliberate you are, the more confident you will look and the more likely you will be to see the notes. When you know what you want to talk about next, look up and make eye contact with a listener. Walk toward that person as you begin to talk about the next point, and continue to look at others as you speak. Repeat as needed.

This sounds simple, but people who first try this often say, "Can I try that again? I looked, but I didn't see anything." The second time they try it, they say, "That really works!"

To do this with perfect confidence, separate each action. Don't talk when you are walking or reading. Look up first, move away from your notes, and then speak. Allow the pauses to create expectation in the minds of your listeners. With a little practice this technique becomes easy to use. Now you never have to worry about forgetting something.

Most speakers find that they need to check their notes less often than they might have thought. You may leave something out, but say it later. The listeners don't know what you planned, so they don't know you made a change.

One good habit is to check your notes occasionally, even if you don't feel at a loss for what to say. This keeps you on track and confident. One last check of your notes before you finish a topic or close your presentation gives you that final opportunity to check for, and add, anything you might not have covered.

Using Visual Aids

Imagine you have made the investment in time and money to travel to a conference. The first speaker's first words are "Before I begin, I want you to know that this entire presentation is available on our Web site."

Still, chances are you will stay to listen, hoping the speaker will add insights, develop the ideas in the slides more fully, or otherwise entertain you. But the speaker asks for the lights to be turned out, turns his back on the audience, faces the screen, and begins to read his slides aloud.

Darkness Makes People Sleepy

We turn lights off when we want to sleep because darkness causes the body to produce melatonin, a hormone that helps make us sleepy. If you want sleepy listeners, turn the lights off. If not, leave the lights on. Ordinary fluorescent lighting is bright enough to inhibit the production of melatonin. Bright light helps keep us wide awake.

So what are your options?

- *Design visual aids so they can be seen in a room that is not completely dark.* The design principles discussed in Chapter 6—high contrast, simplicity, large and legible fonts—help you do this.

- *Use the brightest projector available.* Projectors are bright enough to allow some room light. Can you turn off lights in the front of the room and leave those in the back of the room on? This increases the visibility of your slides without plunging the room into darkness.

- *Try "light breaks."* Design your presentation so you have intervals without slides and turn the lights up during those intervals. Hold intermittent short question-and-answer sessions with the lights on. Encourage your listeners to go outside into the sunshine on breaks.

> **Happiness can be found, even in the darkest of times, if one only remembers to turn on the light.**
>
> ALBUS DUMBLEDORE

The Center of Attention

Are you the center of attention or are your slides? Really think about this. If your slides are intended to visually aid you in the delivery of your message, they are secondary. Can you have the screen put to one side, angled so everyone can see it? If you can, do so. If you can't (if the screen is stationary or can't be moved between speakers), then work to ensure you don't become "the invisible voice in the dark corner."

Changing Slides

These four steps help you use slides as true visual aids.

1. Bring a new slide to the screen.

2. Pause when you introduce a new slide. Do not talk. You should almost always pause when you introduce a new slide. Sometimes you will use your slides as notes. Sometimes you may forget what slide is coming next until you see it. This is not a problem. Let the members of your audience do what they are there to

do: look, think, and learn. Don't chatter on about the slide without letting the audience read it first. When you speak too soon, you create a distraction.

What do you want them to do—read or listen? They can't do both well at the same time. Pause long enough for the audience to take in the visual information visually. A complex slide that needs an immediate explanation is an exception to this rule. Another exception is a quick barrage of slides for special impact. Otherwise, pause. Breathe. Think about what you want to say. Let the slide do its work.

3. Look at the listeners and wait until at least half of the audience looks back at you. Now they are ready to listen. Others will likely finish reading in the next moments.

4. Speak to add value. Do not repeat the words on the slide. The audience just read them. Interpret, explain, and personalize the information on the slides for your audience. You are the expert. What can you tell them that the slide does not already say? Why is the information important to them? If you have nothing else to say, you might as well have emailed them the slides.

The Advantages of Opening and Closing Without Slides

Try opening and closing your presentation without a slide. If speaking at a breakout session at a conference, you may want to have the first slide on the screen as the attendees take their seats. This is one way of helping them make sure they are in the right place. But after that, turn it off. When you start front and center, just you and the audience, you make a much better first impression. You look confident, more conversational, interested in the audience. Do you need the slide competing for the audience's attention as you open your presentation? As you close?

Less is more. Punctuate your presentation with periods of no slides—just one human being talking to others. Remember the Law of Visual Aid Supply and Demand: Every time you add a slide, the other slides become a little less important. Use a slide if it visually aids the listeners' attempts to understand and remember your point. If it doesn't, why do you have it?

Seriously consider closing without a slide. Can the close of the presentation be about the relationship you have built and the action you want? Do you need the slide competing for the audience's attention as you close?

How to Spend a Moment Without a Slide

Are you wondering how to *not* have a slide on the screen during a presentation that includes slides? Read on.

PowerPoint Tips

Some PowerPoint functions can increase the impact of your slides. Use the tips that follow to deliver your message with added expertise.

Befriend Your B Key

If you use PowerPoint or Keynote slides, the B key on your computer's keyboard is a great tool. It allows you to deliver just a visual message, just a spoken message, or both at any time. Try this:

Open a slide presentation. Click on the small screen icon to choose Slide Show format. Press the B key once to blank the screen. Press it again to return to the slide you were on.

Use this simple function to manage your delivery with slides. Blank your screen between slides to cover information that doesn't need visual support, to cover a tangential point, or to answer a question from the audience. Open and close your presentation with a blank screen to give a strong message that you, not your slides, are the expert. This communicates confidence and authority, and increases your ability to quickly establish rapport with your audience.

Navigate by the Numbers

Do you need to return to a particular slide but don't want to take the time to go to slide sorter and then select it? Try this:

1. Open a slide presentation.

2. Choose Slide Show format.

3. Key in the slide number.

4. Hit enter. The slide will appear.

Print a hard copy of your slide sorter before your presentation to have a handy display of all your slides, complete with the corresponding slide numbers. Include it with your speaker notes. You can glance at it, find the slide and slide number, and enter the number.

You are now free to move about the presentation. You can quickly to return to a slide or jump ahead, as you need. No more scrolling through your slides or going back and forth between Slide Sorter and Slide Show while your listeners wait.

PowerPoint and Keynote give you the advantages of a pointer without another piece of physical equipment in your presentation tool chest. If you decide to use this function, practice before your presentation until you can use it easily and comfortably.

A and E

If you use PowerPoint or Keynote slides, the A key on your computer's keyboard will give you a "pointer-on-demand." Try this:

1. Open a slide presentation. Choose Slide Show format.

2. Press the A key once. A small pointer will appear on the screen. You can control the pointer with your mouse. When you are done, press the A key again to remove the pointer from the screen.

3. Right click your mouse. Select *Pointer Options* from the drop-down menu. Click on *Pen*. Your pointer arrow will turn into a small pen icon. Select the color "ink" you want in your pen. Drag your mouse to draw on your slide. This can be useful for circling an area of the slide, underlining for emphasis, and so on. But use this tool selectively—your goal is to direct attention and increase understanding, not to impress the audience with your artistic ability (or even with your proficiency with PowerPoint or Keynote).

4. Erase what you drew by pressing the E key.

For other slide navigation tips, right click your mouse when in Slide Show format. Select Help from the drop-down menu. Spend a few minutes getting familiar with your options.

Pointers

If your slides are simple and clear and the graphics and text are large enough to be seen easily, you will not need a pointer.

Too often pointers are used to give the speaker something to hold onto—something that, if waved, keeps anyone around at a safe distance. Wooden pointers and telescoping metal pointers can be awkward to hold when you're not using them and can look pedantic or authoritarian. If you must use a pointer, don't swing, flourish it, or tap the screen with it. Put it down when you don't need it.

Use a laser light pointer only if you use a large or elevated screen, and only when you need it. You don't want to have the little red light moving all over the screen or shining in the eyes of people in the audience. Holding the light steady on one very small part of the screen is difficult; if you are at all shaky, the light will dance around. Laser pointers work best when used very briefly to circle or pinpoint the detail being discussed. Then turn it off.

Try a Verbal Pointer

Tell the audience where to look and what to focus on. Examples of this technique might include:

- "Let's look at the numbers for January."

- "At the intersection of the two lines we start to see net profit."

Here is a speaker taking his listeners through two slides, using only verbal pointers:

"The pie chart—the one on the left—shows the percentage of market share for the five leading providers at the beginning of the year. We are in blue. Our 27 percent was respectable but certainly not a clear leadership position.

"Now take a good look at the chart on the right. Comparing it to the first shows the progress we made in increasing market share in just the last nine months! Still in blue, we have 37 percent! But now we're in second place.

"Look where we'll be if we grow at this rate for nine months. This slide shows our projected market share by the beginning of third quarter next year. We're still in blue. This pace will give us over 50 percent of the market!"

Lecterns

A lectern distinguishes the speaker from the audience and establishes the speaker as the center of attention. It communicates authority and helps to establish the impression of expertise. It serves another, less obvious purpose as well.

A lectern in the front of the room is like a sturdy tree in an open field—the trunk is protection if vulnerable, exposed, or threatened. Yes, it holds your notes. But so would the slender music stand musicians use to hold their "notes."

A lectern is a barrier between you and the audience. If this suits your purpose, as in

a formal setting with firmly established protocol, then use the lectern. But if you want to eliminate the barrier, as you might if addressing colleagues or potential business partners, it may be better to speak without a lectern or to use it only to hold your notes (as described in the lesson on using notes).

What relationship do you want to have with your audience? Speaking from behind a lectern is a visible way to emphasize the differences between you and the members of your audience, to communicate power and authority, or to establish yourself as an expert.

Do you want to be seen as a partner? If your goal is to connect with your audience, to eliminate obstacles, to remove barriers, then speaking without a lectern will create an atmosphere that is more democratic and cooperative.

If your goal is some combination of these, review the lesson on using notes. It will give you tips for speaking with notes and using the lectern without staying behind it during your entire talk. You and your listeners can have the best of both worlds.

When You Use a Lectern

- *Check the height of the lectern.* The audience should easily see your face and your gestures. If in doubt, call ahead and arrive early to check. If you are less than about five feet six inches tall, you may want to ask for a small, sturdy platform to stand on.

- *Check the lighting.* Make sure that the area around the lectern is well lit from external sources. Lecterns with lights that shine up on your face can make you look like a Halloween mask.

- *Check the front of the lectern.* Lecterns that have the hotel name plastered across the front can turn your talk into an advertisement for sleeping rooms and restaurants. If you are doing a great deal of speaking in hotels, you may want to bring your own version of a "presidential seal" to cover the advertisement on the front of lecterns.

Microphones

Locate any on-site sound technician. Ask for information about the microphone or sound system. You are likely to encounter three types of microphones. (A fourth, less common type is a headset microphone.) The type you use will depend in part on the type of event, the technology available at the site, and the budget.

1. *Fixed microphones* are attached to a lectern or a stationary stand. These are the most limiting.

2. *Handheld microphones* are just that. Many are now cordless.

3. *Lapel microphones* are usually your best choice. Lapel microphones are cordless, and the head of the microphone is small enough to clip to your lapel, blouse, or tie. Slacks, trousers, or a jacket with a pocket will make it easier to find a secure spot for the battery mechanism (often about the size of a deck of cards). Your hands are free to gesture, change note pages, or work with the keyboard of your computer. You have freedom of movement, and even if you speak from behind a lectern, the microphone is the same distance from your mouth at all times, regulating your volume and preventing volume fadeouts. Most venues have lapel microphones available on request.

Using Microphones

- *The head of the microphone should be about six inches from your mouth, pointing at your chin.* Attach a lapel microphone where you won't brush it with your hand or sleeve. If working with a corded microphone, do a run through. Arrange the cord so you will not trip. Hold the microphone in one hand and loop the slack of the cord in your free hand. Practice doing other things, like changing slides or note pages with the other while keeping the microphone the same distance from your mouth.

- *Ask if you will turn the microphone on and off or if this will be done for you.* It is usually done for you, but if not, find the on/off switch and test it. Keep your microphone off until just before your presentation begins. Switch it off again when you are done. If for some reason your microphone must be kept open (in the on position), be very, very aware of what you say and do at all times.

- *Conduct a sound check before the audience arrives.* Any echo will be greater when the room is empty. Rely on the sound technician for advice or an adjustment later. Ask the sound technician about any potential problems with feedback. They may be eliminated if you stay behind any speakers located in the front of the room.

- *Go lightly on the exploding consonants such as p and t.* They can make an annoying popping sound if overemphasized. Avoid audible sniffing and clearing of your throat.

- *Never wear a lapel microphone into the restroom.* No explanation needed.

Teleprompters

Will a speech or presentation be easy if you have a script in front of you? Does knowing that teleprompter technicians are trained to follow you, so the script will move with you as you speak, reassure you as well? Is this the answer to all your worries?

Working with a teleprompter is quite a challenge. Unless you are a skilled actor, reading a script will make you look and sound like you are reading a script. It is difficult to speak naturally, conversationally, in a way that achieves the look and feel of dialogue, when you follow a script.

Ron Burgundy: "That's going to do it for all of us here at Channel 4 news. You stay classy, San Diego. I'm Ron Burgundy?"
Ed Harken: "Damn it! Who typed a question mark on the teleprompter?!"

Reading from a teleprompter makes natural gestures, movement, and facial expressions difficult, and the voice tends to become monotonous. The body often stiffens, and the reliance on the script means you focus on the teleprompter instead of using good eye contact with listeners in all parts of the room. Repeatedly moving your eyes from one side of the screen to the other as you read, while the body does not move naturally, makes it obvious you are dependent on the teleprompter.

It is difficult to write a script that allows for the natural cadences, contractions, and even the structure of spontaneous speech. For many reasons, we do not speak the way we write. If, for legal, political, or business reasons, you must deliver the exact words as they are scripted, a teleprompter may be a good choice. But if choosing your words and structuring your sentences spontaneously will not get you sued, cause an international incident, or result in a market crash, you are better off creating notes as described in Chapter 3 and using them as recommended earlier in this chapter.

Using a Teleprompter

If you will use a teleprompter, here are a few suggestions for using it well.

- *After writing the script, review it out loud several times.* Does the writing sound natural? Are you comfortable with the length and rhythm of the sentences and with the choice of words? Do you really talk that way? If not, change it.

- *Write in contractions as you do when speaking.* Write "don't" rather than "do not," "let's" rather than "let us."

- *Consider writing numbers out.* For example, write "three million, four hundred twenty thousand, eight hundred" instead of 3,420,800. Generally speaking, larger numbers increase the chance of stumbling, especially when the numbers are millions, billions, or beyond.

- *When speaking, do not consistently elongate the vowels in the words "a" and "the."* In conversation, when they precede a word that begins with a consonant, the vowels in both these words are usually pronounced something like the short "u" in "cup," not the long vowel sound we use when reciting the list of vowels as in "a, e, i, o, and u." For example, we pronounce "the" in "the dog" differently than "the" in "the elephant." When reading aloud, some people pronounce every "a" as in "way" and every "the" as "thee." This sounds even more like reading.

- *Remember to pause.* Punctuate your speech with frequent pauses, and use these pauses to look at areas of the audience not in the line of vision with the teleprompter screens. Incorporate gestures, body movement, and facial expressions, and vary your vocal delivery, so you look and sound as natural as possible.

- *Don't shout or overemphasize.* You have a microphone. Don't fall into the style of speakers who increase volume and drama beyond what you need. This is a hangover from the days before microphones, and an overly dramatic delivery style will not sound sincere.

> **Lower your voice and strengthen your argument.**
> LEBANESE PROVERB

Summary

When you make wise choices and use notes, visual aids, lecterns, microphones, and teleprompters skillfully, you have less to worry about and look confident and comfortable.

Notes show thoughtful preparation and a determination to stay focused and give your listeners all the information they need. They insure against memory loss that follows a rise in your cortisol level. Master the pause to use notes well. Feel free to check your notes as often as you need. When you pause long enough to really read your notes, you will look more confident and need to check less often. Resume talking after you have reestablished eye contact with a member of the audience.

Visual aids should help listeners understand and remember information. Add value by explaining, interpreting, personalizing, and reinforcing the message on a visual aid. Pause when you introduce a new visual aid to let it do its work. Look at the audience, not at the visual aid, while you speak.

Lecterns clearly separate you from the audience. Use one to establish authority or expertise, or if the venue or protocol requires it. To create a democratic and cooperative environment, step away from the lectern to speak. Return to it to check your notes or change your slides. Plan ahead to make sure it is positioned appropriately, is the right height, and is lit properly.

Test a microphone ahead of time. Practice with it to make sure you don't fade in and out or produce annoying feedback. Use a clip-on cordless microphone for freedom of motion and freedom from cords. Turn off the microphone when not in use to avoid possible embarrassment.

Use teleprompters only when usual notes won't do. Remember to maintain natural body language, vocal tones, and word choice.

11

It is difficult to keep quiet if you have nothing to do.

ARTHUR SCHOPENHAUER

LET'S JUST TALK

Moving from Monologue to Dialogue

We learn to speak by exchanging words with others—at first one, then two, then phrases and sentences. Dialogue develops between a mother and infant in the first few weeks of the infant's life. This happens quickly and naturally, evidence that the turn-taking of conversation is an innate element of human nature.[53]

As we grow we seldom need to communicate more than a few sentences without comments, interruptions, questions, or other contributions by at least one other person. In turn, we listen, comment, ask questions, and respond to the messages of others.

In Chapter 1 we saw two other elements of dialogue missing from monologue: grounding and entrainment. Both help us connect with listeners, and without them, communication is more difficult. No wonder even a brief return to dialogue can be a welcome change for you and your listeners.

Involved Listeners Are Attentive

In *Grooming, Gossip, and the Evolution of Language*, Professor Robin Dunbar shares observations and conclusions about the human predisposition toward dialogue in small groups. Dunbar describes this behavior as seen at parties and receptions.

Dunbar describes how conversations progress comfortably between two, three, and four people. But when a fifth person joins the small group, the situation gets awkward. Even when members consciously try to involve all five (or more) people in the group, the attention level and interest in the conversation starts to wane. Two people strike up their own conversation, then drift away and start their own group. Dunbar observes, "This is a remarkably robust feature of human conversational behavior, and I guarantee that you will see it if you spend a few minutes watching people in social settings."[54]

If one talks to more than four people, it is an audience; and one cannot really think or exchange thoughts with an audience.

ANNE MORROW LINDBERGH

A large body of research shows that when listeners feel involved, they learn more, remember more, and are more likely to consider new points of view. When listeners feel involved, they are more likely to be persuaded.[55]

The strong human preference for communicating in small groups helps explain why listeners' attention may wander. People stay attentive when they feel involved, even more so when involvement means active participation. When the participation is low, as in groups larger than four, people look for ways to become more actively involved. At cocktail parties they start a new conversation and form a new small group.

So someone who seldom does monologues delivers a presentation to people who prefer dialogue. Skillful speakers understand this and find ways to present with the "look and feel" of dialogue. You learned some ways of accomplishing this in previous chapters. Your content, word choice, delivery style, and use of tools all help.

There are other ways to create the look and feel of dialogue. Try one or two of the ideas below in your next presentation to help the audience stay attentive, and build rapport. The benefits far outweigh the risks.

Here are four things to try.

1. Surprise or startle the audience.

2. Tell a story or share an anecdote.

3. Do something to change the pace of your presentation.

4. Ask audience members to do something that requires a change in the direction of their thinking.

Surprise or Startle the Audience

Let the audience process this information and respond emotionally. Here are some specific suggestions with examples.

- *Give a little-known fact.* "Studies show that companies that increase customer retention by just 5 percent can increase bottom-line profits by as much as 50 percent."

- *Share the latest news.* "This morning, Global Air made an offer to buy Air Express."

- *Make a startling or shocking statement.* "Look around your table. Within seven years, one of you will be dead."

- *Share a startling statistic.* "How pervasive is the information revolution? By 2020, 90 percent of the people in the world more than six years old will have a cell phone."[56]

Tell a Story or Share an Anecdote

You learned about using stories in Chapter 5. Try these types of stories:

- *Share a common experience.* "Last week, driving home from the store, I looked in my rearview mirror and saw flashing red lights."

- *Relate an experience shared by members of the audience.* "When I got here this morning, the parking lot seemed very full. I didn't want to drive to the top of the parking garage, so I pulled up to valet parking…"

- *Share a "learning moment."* "Last night I drove my fourteen-year-old son and three friends home from school. I learned that every one of them is expecting their parents to buy them a car when they turn sixteen!"

Do Something to Change the Pace of Your Presentation

Changing the pace creates a more conversational rhythm. Giving the audience a chance to gather information using a new sense (seeing, hearing, touching, even smelling or tasting)— or using a sense in a new way—is a welcome change. Here are ways to change the pace.

- Use a long pause.

- Use a barrage of statements or facts.

- Do a demonstration.

- Use a series of quick questions.

- Pass out samples.

- Show a single, powerful visual aid.

- Show a short video.

- Use a barrage of visual aids.

- Use a prop.

- Use a series of short statements.

- Ask the audience to do something physical, for example, raise a hand, stand up, look around the room, or shut their eyes.

- Ask the audience to do something intellectual, for example, recall an experience, add some numbers, or guess an answer.

- Ask the audience to imagine something.

- Ask a rhetorical question followed by a long pause.

- Tell the audience to turn to a given page of your handout.

- Tell the audience to make a note of an important point.

Dialogue in Action

Real dialogue will always be the most powerful way to both connect with and learn from your audience. When time, protocol, and your goals allow it, engage listeners in dialogue to connect with them best. Here are ways to encourage dialogue with your listeners.

- *Welcome questions at any time.* When you begin, tell the audience that you will welcome questions at any time. Give them specific directions as to how to let you know they have a question. For example, "As we go through this, let's discuss any questions you have. Whenever you have a question, please raise your hand. I'll call on you as soon as I finish the point I'm on."

- *Hold a question-and-answer session.* When you open your presentation, let the audience know they will have a chance to ask questions. Tell them when this will be and how long it will last. Ask them to make a mental or written note of their questions so they will have them ready when the question-and-answer session begins.

- *Hold intermittent question-and-answer sessions.* If you will speak for longer than about twenty minutes, consider holding brief question-and-answer sessions intermittently. This is a great way to answer questions while they are fresh in the minds of the listeners, and it clears up any confusion that might make it difficult for the listeners to understand the information to follow.

- *Ask for comments.* Asking for comments can be combined with the question-and-answer sessions or done separately and is valuable when you share information without positioning yourself as an expert. Plan to capture shared information by asking a volunteer to record it.

- *Break the audience into small groups to share ideas.* A group of five to eight people usually works best to generate a variety of ideas without becoming unmanageable or encouraging "social loafers" who will let others do all the work. Have a spokesperson from each group report the best ideas back to the larger audience. Clear directions and time limits help this work smoothly.

Avoid the Awkward Silence

Have you ever heard a speaker's question followed by an awkward silence? This attempt to get the audience to participate doesn't always succeed. When a question falls flat, so can the atmosphere in the room. The speaker's confidence can fall, too. The oft-given solution of using an open-ended question (a question that cannot be answered with a yes, no, or very few words) to elicit a longer response such as a description or explanation is not the answer. Here's why.

When a person listens, brain activity increases in certain areas. With the mental shift from listening to preparing to speak, brain activity shifts also. Another shift takes place when the person speaks. These shifts take time, just as a car must slow down to turn a corner, round a curve, or otherwise change direction.[57] A speaker who moves too abruptly from a monologue to a request for a substantive response from the audience is inviting an awkward silence.

If this happens, the awkward silence can be filled in many different ways. Here are some of the steps a speaker can take, along with the pros and cons of each.

Answer the question.

Pro: This fills the awkward silence.

Con: It fails to generate any interaction.

Call on someone specific, i.e., put someone "on the spot."

Pro: The chosen person may rise to the occasion under pressure.

Con: The chosen person can feel anxiety or embarrassment, as may others.

Rephrase the question to be easier to answer.

Pro: This could increase the chances of getting an answer.

Con: It becomes a leading question and sounds manipulative or pedantic.

Pause, wait, and let the tension build.

Pro: Someone may be unable to bear the silence and speak.

Con: Nobody wants to sit through an awkward silence.

Engage-by-Stage to Avoid Falling Flat

To avoid awkward silences and the problems that follow, ask the right kind of question at the right time. Use the *Engage-by-Stage* process to move from monologue to dialogue. The Engage-by-Stage process gives people a chance to move from listening to thinking and then on to speaking, without awkwardness. Each step of the process uses a specific type of question. Asked in order, the questions give listeners a chance to get in touch with their own thoughts, organize those thoughts for speaking, and volunteer to speak when they feel ready. The process is invisible to listeners. With just a little thought you can use it seamlessly. It's fun to use, and the result is real dialogue between you and your listeners. Here are the steps in the process.

Step 1: Ask a Rhetorical Question

Ask a question that is clearly rhetorical. A rhetorical question invites people to think, remember, and call to mind the specifics they need to participate.

An example might be "Think back to the best vacation you had in the last five years. Ask yourself 'What made it good?'"

By saying, "Think back" and "Ask yourself," you identify the question as rhetorical. Nobody should feel a need to speak. Pause and look around the room. Allow time for thought. Observe reactions such as smiles, closed eyes, sighs.

Step 2: Poll with a Show-of-Hands Question

Here's an example: "With a show of hands, how many of you can think of one specific reason why that was such a good vacation?" This show-of-hands question should narrow, focus, and refine their thinking.

Put your own hand up to demonstrate the response you want. This demonstration jump-starts participation. Wait as listeners think, then raise their hands. Some may look around the group, and then be willing to raise their own hands as others do.

Raising their hands increases their involvement. Now they are not only mentally engaged but also physically involved—all in a safe environment. No one person has been singled out, but the show of hands creates a sense of community—many members of the group have things in common. Get a rough count of the response. Is it half the group? More? Everybody? Report the results to the audience. For example, "Okay, it looks like most everybody has a reason." This report will establish a sense of shared experience and interest. Now you and the group are ready for the next step.

Step 3: Ask a "Closed" Question

A "closed" question is one that can be answered very briefly so it makes a response easy. The usual response is yes, no, a number, or a single word or short phrase. This answer is easy for the listeners to supply, especially since they have had time to think. It also is very low risk. It doesn't take much time to organize in their heads. It doesn't demand that the listeners respond articulately or eloquently. It simply breaks the ice and gets them talking out loud. An example might be "Who went with you on that vacation?"

Take several responses so several people have a chance to speak. Probe briefly if necessary or desired; now that they have spoken, you may ask a question to clarify a response. For example, if one of the answers to the question above is "My family," you might ask, "Which members of your family?" or "How many people in all?"

This is the beginning of the real dialogue. When you have had several responses, summarize them. What do the responses have in common? Is there a common thread that should be clarified? An example of a summary might be "It sounds like most of the best vacations were taken with just your spouse." This summary serves as your transition to the next step.

Step 4: Ask an "Open" Question

An "open" question asks the speaker to interpret, elaborate, to describe in further detail, to explain not just the "what" but also the "why." More information is shared, and more opportunities for dialogue emerge. Members of the audience will often discover a shared experience or opinion. Differences of opinion may surface and lead to more dialogue.

An example of an open question might be "What advice would you give to someone planning a vacation with a spouse?" You can go back to the listeners who responded to a question in Step 3, or you may allow anyone in the group to respond.

People will respond. You have created an atmosphere that is safe and participative. You have given listeners time to think about their own experience and learn that others have shared similar experiences.

4. Ask an "open" question.
Facilitate participant responses.
Resist over controlling.

Summarize, move to "goal."

3. Ask a "closed" question.
Take several responses, probe briefly if necessary or desired.

Summarize responses as transition.

2. Poll with a "show of hands" question.
Report the results to the audience to establish a sense of shared experience and interest.

Pause; allow thought, observe reactions.

1. Ask a rhetorical question e.g.:
"Ask yourself this..."
"Think about the last time you..."

then PAUSE; allow thought, observe reactions.

Let the Discussion Flow

Resist the temptation to over control the responses. This is the dialogue you need. Some of the responses and input may be unanticipated, but a free flow of dialogue will yield bits of information you find pertinent and useful. Select the points that advance the discussion and incorporate this information. For example, if your goal is to present a set of guidelines for a successful vacation, you might incorporate information from the dialogue this way: "It sounds like planning activities you both enjoy is key to reconnecting and rekindling that romantic feeling. We also heard how important it is for vacationers to be willing to try something new. Several people said that when they took a risk they had the most fun."

> Communication is not monologue. It is dialogue…The finest art of communication is not learning how to express your thoughts. It is learning how to draw out the thoughts of another.
>
> TEDD TRIPP

Once the dialogue has begun, use your own good judgment to manage it. How long will you let it go on? How many people do you want to hear from? How much detail do you want from each person? How will you manage the dialogue if speakers disagree? How will you summarize the information you get? How will you return to your topic? When you do, how will you incorporate what you have learned?

The answers to these questions depend on the situation. But you will be surprised by how easy it is to manage the dialogue. You may handle it the same way you would managing a meeting.

Your keys to success with the Engage-by-Stage process are:

- Choose your questions thoughtfully.

- Stay open to audience responses that differ from what you expect.

- When you need to, probe for additional information.

- Listen closely to the dialogue for information to further the discussion. Incorporate this information as you summarize the dialogue and return to topic, that is, the topic you planned to cover and the points you planned to make.

Try using the Engage-by-Stage process in a meeting while comfortably seated. Polish the skill of using it to start and manage dialogue. Your meetings will become more participative as you become skillful at asking the appropriate questions, probing effectively for needed details, and guiding the conversations to productive conclusions. And the skills will transfer easily to a more formal presentation environment.

Practicing the Engage-by-Stage process will give you the skill and confidence to move smoothly and comfortably from monologue to dialogue. You will have another great way to make your presentations more interactive, more relaxed, more informative, and more fun!

Summary

We learn to speak using dialogue. The turn-taking of conversation is the basic and most practiced form of speech, while monologue is unnatural and seldom practiced. This can add to our discomfort when we make a presentation and make it difficult for listeners to stay interested and attentive.

Participation is the key to intellectual and emotional involvement. Skillful speakers understand this and create opportunities for dialogue with members of the audience. When this is not possible, they incorporate verbal tools to create the "look and feel" of dialogue.

12

Too much agreement kills a chat.

ELDRIDGE CLEAVER

MEETING OF THE MINDS

Answers to Questions on Questions and Answers

nswering questions can be the best part of your presentation. If your presentation has been a monologue until now, a question-and-answer session starts a dialogue with your audience. And you are a dialogue expert.

A question-and-answer session is an opportunity to work toward understanding and agreement. The audience members can share their thoughts with you. You add details they want, explain in more depth, and have the chance to eliminate confusion or misunderstanding.

You may think the audience will expect you to have all the answers. You may worry that you can't predict all the possible questions, so you can't possibly be prepared with all the perfect answers. Any concerns you have about losing credibility, failing to convince, or simply exposing yourself as less than a total expert may cause anxiety. These are normal concerns, but are they justified?

Remember: A presentation is a chance to share, not an oral exam. Your job is to share what you know and to learn what the audience still needs to know when you handle questions. You will be able to answer many questions on the spot. Sometimes you will refer the questioner to another source, explain why the question can't be answered, or state when it will be. You may need to research some. These are all legitimate options. But let's first look at how to be as prepared as possible.

You Can Prepare for Most Questions

This is because most questions are FAQs (frequently asked questions) and FAQs can be anticipated. Many other questions can also be anticipated. In most cases you have been asked to speak because you know at least as much about your topic as the audience does, and will know most of the answers.

With a little bit of thought, and a little bit of detective work, you can be extremely well prepared for most questions you will be asked.

Brainstorm Possible Questions

Brainstorm a list of questions you might be asked. What would the most supportive members of your audience want to know? The most knowledgeable? The least knowledgeable? The most skeptical? You might be too close to your subject to anticipate some of the simplest questions. Have others brainstorm questions for you. Different perspectives help tremendously in thinking "outside the box."

Now think about and prepare your answers. Do your homework. Contact a few members of your audience. Ask for concerns or questions. If you can't talk to audience members in advance, who has similar interests, concerns, and challenges? What do they want to know? This will give you a list of the most likely questions. But not all the preparation can be done ahead of time. Some preparation takes place after you actually listen to a question.

At Your Presentation

Prepare to Answer

When you get a question, first, be quiet. Nothing will make you look more confident than exercising your right to think for a few moments. Pause and take a breath before you speak. Are you sure you know precisely what is being asked? If not, take steps to make sure you do.

- *Clarify the question.* Perhaps the question is unclear. Do what you would do in a dialogue. If you aren't sure, ask. Ask for a brief explanation, for the context of the question, for a missing essential detail. Ask before you answer the wrong question.

- *Encourage more information.* When you need more information but aren't sure what to ask, use body language and verbal cues to encourage the questioner to continue or expand on the question. A pause with raised eyebrows is usually enough for the questioner to realize you need more information. "Tell me a bit more about what you are thinking" encourages the questioner to give the extra information you need.

- *Mirror the question.* Repeat the question using the questioner's exact words. This is helpful if you think they may have misspoken. Keep your voice neutral—you don't want to sound sarcastic. Mirror the question to check for or to demonstrate understanding, not to stall for time. If you need more time to think, pause.

- *Paraphrase the question.* Paraphrasing (stating the question in your own words) demonstrates how well you understood the question. Paraphrasing gives the listener an opportunity to clarify the question if you have not understood it correctly or fully. This helps you "ground" the exchange of information; to check for understanding. Avoid the overused phrase "So what I'm hearing you say is…" A simple "Do you mean…?" or "Let's see if I got that right…" is better.

- *Repeat the question.* Repeat the question if some members of the audience may not have heard the question the first time. But don't repeat the question just to gain time to think. That technique is more tricky than honest. Pause instead. Don't rush.

The Answer
Easy Questions

You have a ready answer. The answer is not confidential, proprietary, or controversial. Most listeners will likely understand and agree. Often, your biggest challenge is to be brief. Not everyone is likely to want all the details. This is not the time to demonstrate the breadth and depth of your knowledge. It is time to give the questioner the information she needs and move on to the next question.

Hard Questions

You don't have a ready answer. The topic may be controversial, or the information confidential or proprietary. Perhaps it would take a long time to answer, or a complete understanding would require more knowledge than the questioner has. Perhaps the questioner is hostile, argumentative, or is using the opportunity to relate a horror story about an experience they had with your company.

You cannot afford to come across as hostile or argumentative. You have more than this one person to consider; the rest of the listeners are looking to you to have grace under pressure. You

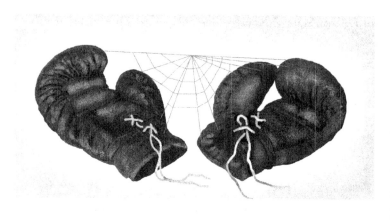

need to put down the gloves and take the high road. And the upper hand.

No matter why the question is difficult, the first thing to do is almost always the same: Pause and think. This will help you respond clearly, and appear knowledgeable, confident, and honest. If you start your answer immediately, you may be sending out a very rough draft. Without taking a few seconds to choose your words, you may need to backtrack or rephrase what you said. You may need more time to explain, qualify, or even apologize.

It isn't always easy. Your instinct will be to immediately start talking. You will feel uncomfortable with the silence of the pause. You may assume that an immediate response demonstrates knowledge, while a pause sounds as if you don't know the answer.

Will pausing give the impression that you don't know the answer? No. When you pause, with confident and non-defensive body language, you look thoughtful and confident. The impressions you create are these:

- I am genuinely considering what you have asked.

- I am thinking about how best to respond to meet your needs.

- I am comfortable being here.

- I believe this is an opportunity to share information and understand one another, not an oral exam.

- My answer will be worth the short wait.

Maintain eye contact with the questioner, and a friendly or neutral expression, as you pause. Resist the natural impulse to look or walk away from the questioner.

The Model Answer

These three steps help you construct an answer that will satisfy the person who asked the question, other listeners, and you. As you become more skillful in using this model you will be able to think of excellent answers to hard questions in the moment—not on the way home. The three steps are:

1. Find common ground.

2. Give the substance of your answer. Add to, clarify, or explain your reasoning, content, or position.

3. Restate your belief, opinion, or recommendation or an important point.

Step 1: Find common ground.

What can you and the questioner agree on? For example, if the question lets you know a customer is balking at the price you quoted, you can agree on the fact that "Price will certainly be an important part of your decision."

Responding with "I understand what you mean, but…" does not prove you understand. It does not establish common ground. This well-worn phrase sounds like you assume you understand, you disagree, and you can't wait to say why.

Common ground can almost always be found in a major issue common to business—and life. We all seek trust, fairness, dependability, reliability, cost effectiveness, experience, skill, communication, and other basics in others and in products, services. The vast majority of tough questions have one of these major issues at their core. What issue is at the core of the question?

Sometimes the only common ground is "This is a really tough issue, and we both definitely have strong feelings about it!" But finding some common ground is a great way to immediately create a feeling of working with questioners, not against them. When you have established common ground, begin the substance of your answer.

Step 2: Give the substance of your answer.

Add to, clarify, or explain your reasoning, content, or position. What else should the listeners know? What details are needed? Give this information as succinctly as you can.

Clarify or correct understanding. When a question shows misunderstanding of the information, you have the opportunity to clarify or correct it. Sharing information that may contradict or rebut that of the questioner without causing conflict can make all the difference.

Explain your reasoning. Describe how you arrived at your position. Explain the factors you considered when making it, the advantages and disadvantages, the expected short- and long-term results. Show that the advantages outweigh the disadvantages.

Step 3: Restate your belief, opinion, recommendation, or point.

As you finish your answer, reset your course by repeating an important point you want the listeners to remember. This is a great way to refocus yourself and the audience on the content and purpose of your presentation, not on the last question.

Choosing Not to Answer

Just because someone asked you a question doesn't mean that you must answer. Is the answer within the scope of your expertise, or is someone else better qualified to answer the question?

My best attribute is knowing when not to answer stupid questions.
GINA GERSHON

Should you answer it at all? Some questions are so unrelated to the topic that answering them would waste everyone else's time. Some don't have an answer. It may be impossible to state definitively, be a matter of opinion, or be unknown. It may be confidential or proprietary.

In a presidential debate, Ohio Governor John Kasich responded to a question about whether another candidate was naïve with "I'm not going to bite." There was enthusiastic applause from an audience clearly tired of personal attacks and lightweight questions. Kasich then went on to talk about international policy.[58]

When You Don't Know the Answer

If you believe you should know the answer but don't, you can offer to find out and then get back to the questioner. Choose this option when you are the best source of an answer, and get the questioner's contact information or give yours before leaving.

But you can't read every story, and answer every question even if you'd like to.
LEMONY SNICKET

If the answer is outside your scope of knowledge or responsibility, say so. Refer the questioner to another source for the answer. The best source may be a reference document, an internet search, or another person.

It may be appropriate to ask "Can anyone here answer that question?" or "Has anyone here faced that issue?" If you choose this approach, be prepared. You might not agree with the answer. You might get a long-winded volunteer and have to manage the length of the answer. But it may also be a great way to get the audience involved.

Questions Unrelated to the Topic

Some questions are unrelated to the topic, only superficially related, or so specific to the questioner that answering them would waste the time of the rest of the listeners. When you get this kind of question, it is your responsibility to redirect the group back to the topic at hand. For example, "That is interesting as well. Come up after we finish if you'd like to talk about that with me. In the time we have left I need to answer as many questions directly related to our topic as I can. What other questions do we have?"

Confidential and Proprietary Information

If the question involves proprietary or confidential information, say so. But "No comment" sounds evasive. Instead, tell the audience what you can say, and let them know if and when you will be able to say more. It might sound something like this: "That information is proprietary. I can say we are aware of needs in that area. We're working hard on this issue and hope to have a related announcement before the end of the third quarter."

Questions Already Answered

Be willing to repeat information you already covered. If one person missed some of the earlier information, the chances are other members of the audience also missed it. Don't begin your answer with "As I said earlier," or anything to that effect; it can sound as if you are chastising the questioner. Instead, make a mental note of it. Could you present it in a clearer or more memorable way the next time?

Rarely, someone may repeatedly ask questions on material you already covered. If repeating these answers would not be a good use of time for others in the audience, you may choose to offer to meet with the questioner after your talk or to send them the information. Then move on to give others a chance to ask questions.

Hostile and Argumentative Questions

To answer a hostile question, follow the three steps for framing an answer.

Become familiar with the logical fallacies covered in Chapter 13. Many tough and hostile questions, and all trick questions, contain a logical fallacy. When you recognize the fallacy, you respond more easily, confidently, and effectively. When you respond calmly

> **There is nothing more exhilarating than to be shot at without result.**
> WINSTON CHURCHILL

and logically, you can defuse a potentially damaging situation and increase your credibility.

A hostile questioner is less likely to engage when they realize their own faulty thinking will be clearly and publicly exposed.

The Controlling Questioner

A controlling questioner may attempt to dominate by shouting his question without regard for protocol, ask multiple questions, or try to argue. If the questioner attempts to dominate by shouting a question, try this. Look the person in the eye and calmly say, "Please remember that question. Let me finish this answer and I'll get back to you shortly." Then turn away and proceed with the answer you choose. This action will reinforce the protocol and your authority and will show respect for the other listeners. Return to the questioner when it is appropriate to do so.

If one questioner insists on asking multiple questions, be firm. Answer what you think you should and then say something like "I want to answer the questions of as many people as possible. Who else has a question?" Look away from the controlling questioner as you speak, and make eye contact with other listeners as a way of inviting their questions.

If the questioner attempts to draw you into a discussion that is inappropriate for the situation, you may need to take the question "off-line." Try something like this. "I need to know the specifics of your situation. Right now I need to answer as many questions as I can in the time we have. Come up when we're finished here and we can talk about it one-on-one." Then make eye contact with someone else as you ask, "Who has the next question?"

Technical Questions

Nontechnical people complain that technical people give too much information and too many details when asked a question—"I asked what time it was, and got instructions on how to build an atomic clock!"

Someone told me that each equation I included in the book would halve the sales.
STEPHEN HAWKING

Excessive information frustrates a less technical questioner and wastes time. It reduces the number of questions you take in the limited time available. Yet a specialist or technical presenter, understanding the many variables that can complicate an issue and wanting to be precise, thorough, truthful, and helpful, can find it difficult to know when to stop. So how does a technical presenter know how much is enough and when it becomes too much?

In *Effective Communication Skills for Scientific and Technical Professionals*, author Harry E.

Chambers suggests that the technical speaker ask the questioner for guidance. This helps the speaker resolve the "how much detail?" dilemma before beginning the answer. Giving the questioner specific choices about the level of detail wanted can help solve this problem. Paraphrased from Chambers' book, the options might sound something like these:

- "It would help me to know how best to answer that question if I understood more about how you will use the information. Can you tell me more about your need or concern?"

- "I can give you a detailed explanation of the research project—that will take about ten minutes. Or I can give a basic understanding of the design and approach, and tell you how to get more information if you need it."

- "Should I give you a brief overview, and then answer your specific questions?"[59]

If time and protocol allow, the speaker can also offer to answer questions after the presentation, give information such as business cards and email addresses so the questioner can follow up, or allow the rest of the audience to have input on how much time—and interest—they have.

Questions from Top Executives

Top executives are likely to ask two types of questions: extremely high level or very precise and detailed. The high-level questions are often the questions that have to do with the larger organizational strategy, while the precise and detailed questions address the orchestration, implementation, and specifics of the expected results. Here's an example of a high-level question: "What do you believe are the implications of this reorganization in light of our emphasis on R and D?"

An example of an extremely precise question is this: "How would the key numbers change if that interest rate rises by 2 percent?"

To prepare for an executive presentation, think through the types of strategic and implementation challenges related to your topic. While it would be wonderful if you could have all the answers on the tip of your tongue, you can't. No one can. But answers that show you considered the high-level strategy issues demonstrate that you have basic business sense. Showing you considered various approaches and options related to organizational strategy demonstrates flexible thinking and open-mindedness and enhances credibility more than giving vast amounts of detail or being able to answer every question on the spot.

This is doubly true if the questions are hypothetical. And if the detailed question is hypothetical, especially when it requires that you "crunch numbers" to provide a specific answer, the math can be done.

Use Consistent Body Language

When you answer questions, use the same body language as before. A noticeable style change between the different parts of your presentation raises questions about your credibility—if you were "real" only part of the time, when were you real, when weren't you, and what were your intentions?

Even the best answer loses credibility if answered in a defensive or evasive way. Answers that may not completely satisfy a listener are more easily accepted if answered in a straightforward and confident way. While body language is no substitute for knowledge of content, your behavior when answering a question is an important part of the total message you communicate.

Awareness of how the body responds to stress, and how to use body language to support your content, are important parts of delivering your message. Without this knowledge, feelings of anxiety or stress will show in your body language. With this knowledge your body language can communicate confidence and sincerity. Knowing you look and sound confident will allow you to relax and think clearly. The nonverbal delivery skills introduced in Chapter 8—pace and pause, eye contact, posture, facial expressions, voice, gestures, and movement—will all serve you well.

Pause and Breathe

You know it is important to pause before you begin an answer. Be sure you remember to breathe while you pause. Holding your breath will make you feel and look tense. And don't exhale audibly. You don't want to sigh out loud as you think about what to say.

Maintain Eye Contact

Eye contact is extremely important when answering questions. Maintain eye contact with each questioner as they speak. Even if looking away feels more comfortable, it will almost always give the impression that you are not listening. With eye contact you can see facial expressions or body language that give clues about the questions behind the question. If you absolutely must look away to think, look back and reestablish eye contact with the listener before you begin speaking. Don't deliver your answer to the floor, wall, or ceiling—deliver it to the questioner. If the answer is very brief, you can maintain eye contact with the questioner throughout your delivery. If the answer is lengthier—if it lasts much more than about ten seconds, it is often best to look at others in different parts of the audience as you continue with your answer. Too much eye contact with the questioner can become uncomfortable for both parties. It will also weaken your connection with others who are interested and should be included. Some members of the audience may not be as interested; eye contact will help them stay attentive.

End the answer with confidence. When you move your eyes off the questioner and include others in the answer, you can choose whom you want to have eye contact with as you finish. You will be inclined to look back at the original questioner as you conclude to check for facial expressions and body language that communicate understanding and acceptance of your answer. In presentations that aim to educate or inform the audience, you may want to ask, "Does that answer your question?"

Ending the Answer to a Hostile Question

Don't look back. If the questioner is argumentative or hostile, you can choose not to look at them again as you complete your answer. This reduces the chance that the questioner will ask another question or try to embroil you in an argument. It gives a strong message that the topic has been dealt with and you are ready to move on to the next question. A powerful democratic dynamic exists in most question-and-answer sessions. Most listeners accept that other listeners must also be given a chance to ask questions.

Closing the Question-and-Answer Session

Keep track of the time while answering questions. Ask for help with this if you need it. Find someone—even a member of the audience—who will keep track of the time and let you know several minutes before time is up. Then let the audience know you have time for just one or two more questions. You may want to invite one-on-one questions after the presentation.

Summary

Answering questions can be the best part of your presentation. Question-and-answer sessions start a dialogue with your audience, and you are a dialogue expert. You learn the most with dialogue. The audience members can share their thoughts with you. You can learn about their concerns, add details they want, explain in more depth, and you have the chance to eliminate confusion or misunderstanding.

To make the most of a question-and-answer session, brainstorm a list of possible questions.

Then identify which can be easily answered, which need to be researched, and which may need to be referred or deferred. A presentation is a chance to share, not an oral exam. Your job is to share what you know and learn what the audience still needs to know.

The three-step model for framing your answers can be used for planning answers to anticipated questions and for thinking on your feet as you respond to unanticipated questions. The three steps are:

1. Find common ground.

2. Give the substance of your answer. Add to, clarify, or explain your reasoning, content, or position.

3. Restate your belief, opinion, recommendation, or an important point.

Use body language that communicates confidence, honesty, and a sincere desire to share information with the audience.

Conclude your presentation by restating the close of your prepared remarks, and then stand in place for a few seconds. Enjoy the applause!

13

Nothing is as frustrating as arguing with someone
who knows what he's talking about.

SAM EWING

SOMETHING ISN'T RIGHT HERE

Recognize and Rout Trick Questions

Many tough questions, especially trick questions, contain logical fallacies. A fallacy is an argument that sounds convincing but is essentially flawed. The ability to recognize fallacies is an immensely important skill for speakers in highly visible, controversial, and high-stakes situations.

Fallacies are usually born from an attempt to persuade through illogical means, but can also be caused by careless thinking. Professional interviewers, including business and financial analysts, can be skilled at asking questions that contain fallacies. These questions sound persuasive and are difficult to answer well if you can't recognize and expose the logical flaw.

When listeners ask us tough questions, fallacies in our own arguments are vulnerable to exposure. We can make an argument that sounds persuasive but might be wrong for any number of reasons. Our "facts" might be wrong or incomplete. We can be wrong about what we have inferred and concluded. We may use words carelessly. Or we may use words in clever ways in an attempt to influence our listeners in an illogical way.

When familiar with the most common fallacies, we are unlikely to commit them unconsciously. If you leave yourself open to having your faulty thinking exposed in a public forum, you should at least do it consciously!

An explanation of the logical fallacies often found in tough questions asked at business presentations follows. Each fallacious argument is identified, defined, and then used in a sample question similar to one you might hear at a presentation. The first six fallacies include not only sample questions but also sample answers that debunk the fallacious argument.

To practice handling tough questions, try constructing the answers to the remaining sample questions yourself. Remember to consider the tone of your answer as well as the content. It will be helpful to refer to the three-step model for framing your answers that was introduced in the last chapter.

Common Fallacious Arguments

Begging the Question

It has become common for the phrase "begs the question" to be mistakenly substituted for "raises the question," but these two phrases have very different meanings. Begging the question is also known as assuming the answer or circular reasoning. This fallacy occurs when a proposition is used to prove itself. It may sound as if the speaker is giving a reason for something when she is simply restating it. In more formal terms, when the premises in an argument for a proposition contain the proposition itself, both are equally doubtful.

Question: "Since the best way to improve customer satisfaction is to inspect the finished products twice, can't we try doubling the number of inspections on the finished product?"

Answer: "Nobody wants defective products leaving the factory. But the cost of producing a defective product remains even if we catch it before it is shipped. Let's think about ways to reduce the number of defects happening."

Loaded Question

A loaded question includes an assumption as an attempt to damage the position of the other party. This sidetracks the argument. It can antagonize others by making them feel manipulated or bullied.

Question: "We know how weak the marketing department is. Don't you think someone on the development team should write the press release?"

Answer: "The development team will have input on what should be included in the press releases. The marketing people have their challenges. The timing of our competitors' last releases and budget restraints makes things tough. They did a good job with other press releases, and writing them will still be their responsibility."

Swinging the Big Stick

Swinging the big stick is more formally known as the argument from adverse consequences or the appeal to fear. The threat of harm is used to advance the speaker's position.

Question: "How can we not raise our prices? If we don't raise prices, we won't make any money this year. No raises, no bonuses, and no job security next year."

Answer: "We will need to look at ways to improve the bottom line. One idea is to establish whether a drop in prices would increase sales volume enough to improve the bottom line. Another is to look for ways to cut expenses."

Slippery Slope

The slippery slope fallacy assumes that if a first step is taken, an inevitable and disastrous set of consequences will follow. These consequences are given as the reason for not taking the first step. The slippery slope assumes an inability to make exceptions, set limits, or make decisions on a case-by-case basis.

Question: "Do you think this is wise? If we fund this project, pretty soon we're going to have all our engineers working on their own ideas, no matter how unlikely they are to ever generate revenue, and then key projects will never be completed!"

Answer: "We have criteria for funding, including potential payoff. We can make each call based on the criteria, just as we do every time we approve a budget or target potential customers."

C Cubed

C cubed—the confusion of correlation and causation—is also known as the fallacy of false cause. It assumes that because two events happened together—in time, in place, or to the same person or group—one must have caused the other.

Question: "When the stock markets peaked, our national murder rate dropped faster and farther than any time in the last thirty-five years. How can you doubt that prosperity lowers crime rates?"

Answer: "We were both happy with the drop in crime then. I'm even happier that we haven't seen violent crime rates rise in spite of the recession and the slow recovery. Some sociologists attribute the drop in violent crime to a change in policing policies in major cities. Some think it is due more to an aging population and the resulting drop in testosterone levels! It's probably a combination of factors."

Non Sequitur

Non sequitur is Latin for "it doesn't follow." A non sequitur is an error in logic made when the conclusion of an argument fails to follow from its premise or premises.

Question: "Why should we worry so much about maintaining market leadership? We have by far the best quality products. Our users love us!"

Answer: "There's no doubt our quality helps us hold onto our market leadership. Recently we have been hearing more customers begin to question our pricing. They say that some competitors have products that work well for them and are priced well below ours. Let's talk about how customers make buying decisions."

Straw Man

The straw man fallacy is used when a person attacks an argument different from and weaker than the opposition's best argument. This is often done by caricaturing the opposition as so extreme in his views as to be ridiculous—by creating a "straw man" to attack.

Question: "So now a customer who wants us to hold their hands twenty-four hours a day—troubleshoot process for them, train their staff for them—wants us to give them new software for practically nothing? And you think we should be grateful for the chance to do it?"

How would you answer?

Post Hoc, Ergo Propter Hoc

Post hoc, ergo propter hoc is Latin for "it happened after, so it was caused by." It is often referred to as simply post hoc. This error is committed when one assumes that because something happened after something else, the first event caused the second.

Question: "Last January we reorganized the sales teams, and sales rose 15 percent for the first two quarters. Shuffling players must reinvigorate the sales force. When should we reorganize again?"

How would you answer?

False Dichotomy

This is also known as false dilemma or excluded middle. It presents only two options, usually extremes, when more options exist. It implies that other options or compromise solutions are not possible. The bumper sticker classic is "America—love it or leave it."

Question: "If we can't dominate that market, there's no point. Let's dump that division before it starts to be a financial drain! Then we can focus our resources."

How would you answer?

Short Term versus Long Term

Short term versus long term is an especially common form of the false dilemma.

Question: "How can you recommend *any* increase in R&D spending when Wall Street is howling about our last earnings projection?"

How would you answer?

Appeal to Ignorance

The appeal to ignorance assumes that whatever has not been proved false must be true and vice versa.

Question: "Metal fatigue can't be ruled out. Let's investigate that first."

How would you answer?

> I mean, you could claim that *anything's* real if the only basis for believing in it is that nobody's proved it doesn't exist!
>
> HERMIONE GRANGER

Ad Hominem

Ad hominem is Latin for "to the man." This happens when a speaker responds to an argument with a comment about the person making the argument, not the argument's merit. Positive or negative, the comment is usually irrelevant to the argument.

Question: "Isn't that the lawyer who got lost on the way here? Why should we hire someone who can't find the way to work?"

How would you answer?

Hasty Generalization

The fallacy of hasty generalization happens when a generalization is induced using a sample that is too small to be conclusive. You've probably heard it called "jumping to a conclusion."

Question: "That was the fourth customer today who bought that book. Do you think we should order a couple hundred to get us through the month?"

How would you answer?

> Based on this one experience I had, jumping to conclusions is always really stupid.
>
> CRAIG BENZINE

Unrepresentative Sample

This error occurs when the sample used, even if quite large, is not representative of the population as a whole.

Question: "Everyone I know—in my neighborhood, at the country club, at the spa—said they were going to vote for Perry. How can Martine be the new mayor?"

How would you answer?

Going Shopping

Going shopping is also known as pick and choose. Going shopping includes two closely related fallacies: observational selection and the fallacy of exclusion. Observational selection means counting the "hits" and not the "misses." Exclusion means not counting the "misses."

Question: "Wow! The California outlets are really doing well. Almost a third of them might make their sales goals. Maybe that son of mine should be a regional manager! Do you think he's ready to supervise Arizona and Nevada, too?"

How would you answer?

False Analogy

The false analogy compares two very different things, states or implies that they are similar, and draws a conclusion about one based on the other. It becomes confusing when the two things may in some way be similar; recognizing the fallacy depends on seeing the differences clearly.

Question: "In both cases, the result is death and mayhem. What's the difference? Selling a car to a teenager is like giving a loaded handgun to a toddler!"

How would you answer?

Popularity

A fallacy of popularity argues that something is true because it is believed to be true by so many people rather than because it has merit.

Question: "Don't you think the way to lose weight is to cut out fat? Look at all the low fat products in grocery stores!"

How would you answer?

Appeal to Authority

The appeal to authority fallacy claims something is true because an authority says so, not because the argument has merit. An authority might be wrong. Experts in the field may disagree, or the authority may be misinformed, misquoted, bribed, or joking. And what is the definition of an authority or expert? As the expansion of knowledge continues and fields become narrower and deeper, an expert in the exact area in question may be harder and harder to find. Perhaps the expert is actually an expert in a different field!

Question: "They're all CPAs. They work for a major firm. They must be right."

How would you answer?

Wrong-Way Street

A wrong-way street occurs when an effect is assumed to be a cause or a cause is assumed to be an effect. This often happens because of limited perspective.

Question: "But we have to keep hiring! If we slow down, we can't keep producing more. How can we keep building sales if we don't increase production?"

How would you answer?

Prejudicial Language

This fallacy implies that ethical or moral goodness is associated with agreeing with the argument. It often uses emotional or value-laden terms to accomplish this.

Question: "So, the generous among us will certainly welcome this opportunity to fulfill our obligation to give back to our community by supporting the selfless work of the tireless and saintly volunteers of this noble charity. Who among you could refuse to do your part?"

How would you answer?

Red Herring

The red herring sounds like it is relevant to the question or topic being discussed but is actually irrelevant. It can throw listeners off track, confuse the issue, and make it harder to reach an agreement and a conclusion.

Question: "Before we ask cities to reduce their water use, shouldn't we know how much fresh water is locked in subglacial reservoirs?"

How would you answer?

The ability to recognize the fallacy in a tough or argumentative question is the first step in being able to respond successfully. But remember, many situations are complex and emotional. What may seem reasonable and logical to you may not be to others.

Peace rules the day, where reason rules the mind.

WILLIAM COLLINS

Summary

Many tough questions and trick questions contain logical fallacies. The ability to recognize and respond logically to fallacious arguments (arguments that may sound convincing but are logically flawed) is an important skill for speakers.

These questions are much easier to answer convincingly when you recognize and expose the logical flaw.

Fallacies in our own arguments are vulnerable to exposure. A familiarity with common fallacies makes us less vulnerable to committing them.

14

LET'S ALL GET TOGETHER

Web Presentations and Second Languages

The Web—the technology needed to communicate over distances—complicates matters. As with in-person presentations the format can vary.

A Web conference usually includes a small group—as few as two people to a maximum of about ten. Opportunities for all participants to speak are the norm. Interaction is expected, making a Web conference an alternative to business meetings.

A webinar, like a seminar, is often associated with training or teaching. It may include just a few participants or many. A webinar may include an opportunity for real-time interaction, for interaction during parts of the event, or for no interaction. As the size of the audience grows, the opportunities for input, interaction, and questions by each individual shrink.

A webcast usually means a presentation via the Web to a large group of people with little or no interaction. Think broadcast.

Define and Assign Roles and Responsibilities

Preparing and delivering a Web presentation demands many individual skills. At times, the presenter will be responsible for any combination of these different tasks. It is a rare person who is highly skilled at all these tasks, or has the time or inclination to handle all of them.

Decide which skills you have, what tasks you can and should handle, and what to delegate.

Dividing tasks allows each to be performed by the person best equipped to do so, while giving them the freedom to focus on what they do best. You may well take on more than one of these roles, but don't be reluctant to state your needs. Get the help you want and need. It can mean the difference between a great Web presentation and a not-so-great one.

- The administrator schedules the conference and coordinates the work of all involved.

- The marketer publicizes and promotes the event.

- The writer/designer determines content and designs the methods of delivery.

- The moderator assists with introductions, facilitates interaction, monitors timing, and follows up.

- The presenter delivers the information to the audience.

- The technician provides technical assistance with preparation and troubleshooting.

When You Administer

If you use a hosting company, contact them as soon as possible to schedule the conference. Schedule additional time in case the presentation runs over the allotted time. Communicate early and often. A schedule and a checklist will help you execute the conference successfully.

Assign the roles above—marketer, designer, moderator, presenter, and technician—appropriately, and encourage people in the different roles to consult one another for any advice and assistance they may need. Check periodically to ensure all the other people handling the rest of the above roles are communicating and cooperating as needed.

When You Market

Identify the desired participants. If possible, use the conferencing tools to invite them, and do this well in advance. Include information they need to participate such as the RSVP method, call-in number, conference link and access code, and any pre-work.

Send occasional reminders in the days or weeks before the event. Include numbers and codes in each reminder. Resend any numbers or codes participants will need the day before the conference. Encourage the attendees to perform a browser check and enter the conference early.

When You Design

Decide what you need and want to accomplish. Be realistic about what you can cover in the time you have. Rushing or leaving material uncovered does not create a good impression.

Plan frequent interaction to change the pace and keep participants interested. Design for some interaction with the audience after about three slides. The interactivity will take time; plan accordingly. Some design elements you might use include:

- Pre-work such as surveys, questionnaires, or self-assessments

- Online introductions

- Online polls

- Problem-solving exercises

- Online brainstorming, categorizing, and setting priorities

- Partner or small group exercises

When You Present

Many of the techniques and skills that work well for a traditional in-person presentation work well for a Web presentation, but the separation inherent in Web presentations complicates the event. Communicate with people handling the other roles to make sure you get what you need.

- Run a dress rehearsal well in advance. Check that your presentation loads correctly far enough in advance to address any problems. Practice with the appropriate software tools to become proficient and comfortable and to discover any problems, confusions, or glitches. Get help or make any changes you need.

- Record your presentation for your own advance review. Time it to make sure it can be completed in the time allowed.

- Learn whether your system allows you to select a full-screen view for your listeners. If so, consider doing so to reduce distractions caused when they view multiple screens at once. Learn to mute or unmute your participants. You may need to.

- Open the conference software well before the start of the presentation. Check all connections and tools, and double-check that content works the way you planned.

- After the conference, send any promised material as soon as possible. Send a thank-you and a survey to all participants.

- Learn how to capture your presentation in its entirety (integrated audio and video) for later review. Reviewing it later is great feedback for you, and you will have it to send to others who could not participate.

When You Moderate

Your role is crucial for an effective Web presentation. Spend the time you need with the presenter, the content, and the technology to help make the conference a success.

- Put in enough practice time to master the conferencing system and tools. Become familiar enough with the material that you can anticipate the need for actions on your part.

- Remove as many unknowns as possible from the minds of the participants. Introduce the presentation, set the protocol, and introduce participants, including each participant's role and location. Explain if, when, and how participation will take place.

- If participants interact by voice, identify each by name and location. If questions or comments are typed and displayed on-screen, especially multiple comments on the same screen, you may need to identify the source of the comment.

When You Provide Technical Support

- Know that the presenter will have challenges, both foreseen and unforeseen. Your support can make or break a presentation.

- Know and trust your system and software. Complete a system and browser compatibility check at least twenty-four hours before your conference. Make sure you have a strong and stable internet connection. If possible, use a wired network connection and switch off wireless on your computer.

- Have an extra computer near you to log in as a participant. Now you can see what participants see, plus you have an extra computer for emergencies.

Bandwidth Is Key

Each participant should receive the same content at the same time. Adjusting for this problem during the presentation—explaining the problem, waiting for everyone to catch up, repeating information—makes the presentation more difficult to deliver, manage, and receive. Lower bandwidth whenever possible to reduce taxing your system so all information is transmitted smoothly. With too little bandwidth, the participants will literally not be on the same wavelength.

Remind participants to close all unnecessary applications on their computers so software operates efficiently. Suggest participants lower their screen resolution to reduce bandwidth and move more quickly through changes.

Keep the room background simple and uncluttered. Solid colors—in the room around you and in your clothing—will be less distracting than patterns and will require less digital data for transmission, helping to maintain the quality of the video.

Audio

Planning and testing in advance are keys to knowing that your audio will be available and clear.

Telephone landlines are still best for high-quality audio. If speaking through the internet, check that all participants have connections fast enough to carry the audio transmission clearly, even at high-traffic periods of the day.

Use a headset rather than your computer's microphone and speakers for the best audio quality. Wearing a headset when using a keyboard or physically managing other elements during the webcast leaves your hands free to handle whatever else you must do.

Video

As with in-person presentations, your listeners will be influenced by what they see before you begin to speak.

Fluorescent lighting can be unflattering. Overhead lighting can make you look scary. The best lighting will be full spectrum for both brightness and warmth and will come from a variety of directions to eliminate shadows. This type of cross lighting may require stage lighting or portable spotlights.

Dress conservatively to keep the focus on your face. Colors that contrast with the background make it easier to see you.

Slides

The recommendations in Chapter 7 help you avoid common mistakes in slide designs. The advice on limiting text, using images, managing necessary detail, and choice of fonts and colors still apply. Yet, some changes, additions, and recommendations will help make sure your slides are best suited for a Web conference.

Put the slide numbers on each slide, in a font large enough to be easily read by participants. This helps them navigate during the conference.

Begin with a welcome slide with enough information so those logging on will know they are in the right "place."

Close with a slide with contact and follow-up information.

Delivery

As with in-person presentations, much of the meaning will come from your tone of voice, inflections, and pauses. But when your listeners can't see you, your speech patterns and the quality of your voice become even more important. Remember to use the vocal delivery skills and the pacing and pausing skills covered in Chapter 9.

Participate from a quiet room. Post a note on your door to let people know that you should not be disturbed, and take any other steps to discourage interruptions—notice to staff, silence phone ringtones, etc.

Keep in mind that the audience can't see everything you see. Avoid gesturing toward your visual aids. And remember to smile. It can warm up an already cool medium, and a smile can be heard as well as seen.

Etiquette Basics

Understanding the etiquette, as speaker or participant, makes everything go more smoothly for all.

Do:

- Be courteous to all.

- Speak clearly. This often means slowing your speech a bit.

- Choose vocabulary all participants will understand.

- If using video, a waist-up shot is generally best. Avoid an extreme close-up headshot.

- Keep body movements minimal.

- Gesture naturally. If you tend to use frequent, exuberant gestures, consider toning them down.

- Both the presenter and the participants should maintain eye contact by looking into the camera.

- Don't shift your weight. Reducing animation keeps you from bouncing around on the screen.

- Dress appropriately.

Don't:

- Make distracting sounds.

- Shout. Extra volume may not help someone understand. Rephrase, explain, or give an example.

- Interrupt other speakers.

- Carry on side conversations.

- Shift your weight or rock in your chair frequently.

- Wear noisy jewelry.

- Cover the microphone.

Language Challenges

Electronic technology is only one way the world continues to become smaller. In a global economy, talent and resources are shared across borders. This means we work with people who speak languages other than the one we are most comfortable with. The following tips can help achieve understanding among people of different backgrounds and talents. Although these tips apply to speakers of English, the principles can be applied to speakers of other languages as well.

> **Do you know what a foreign accent is? It's a sign of bravery.**
> AMY CHUA

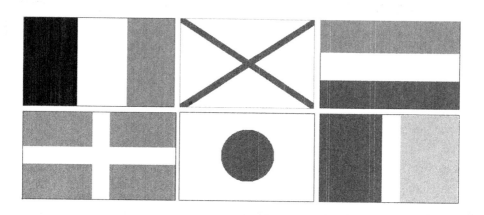

When English Is a Second Language

Many highly skilled members of top organizations speak English as a second or third language. Their technical skills and ability to write may not be matched by their ability to be understood when speaking English.

An accent can be an excellent way to get and keep the attention of listeners, who may be intrigued by the different sound and rhythm. But an accent so strong that it interferes with the speaker's ability to be understood is not an asset. Differences in the sounds, intonations, and stress patterns between English and other languages contribute to the challenge of communicating clearly in a second language.

For example, English tends to stress only one word in a phrase. Stressing more than one, a common pattern in some languages, can create the impression among American listeners that the speaker is irritated or even angry. English also tends to stress the more important words, such as nouns and verbs, and reduce the emphasis on the less important ones. This creates an up-and-down pattern rather than one that is staccato or flat. Consider the following sentence: They *went* to the *zoo* to *study* the *snakes*. A native speaker of English would likely emphasize the words in italics.

In other languages the intonation pattern is often different, creating unintended impressions among listeners who are native speakers of English. Vietnamese, which contains single-syllable words spoken in as many as six different tones, can sound like shouting to the American ear. South Asian speakers, although coming from an area with many different dialects, often speak English without stressing nouns or verbs and with an upward intonation at the end of sentences. To the American ear, this can be interpreted as a questioning tone. Similar to the phenomenon known as "up talk," this can also be interpreted as lacking in confidence and authority.

Accent reduction classes can help speakers of English as a second language identify and practice the sounds and the stress patterns of English. Offered through corporate universities, community colleges, university extension programs, and private companies, an accent reduction class can be an excellent way to improve one's ability to be fully understood by native speakers.

Best Practices for Speakers of English as a Second Language

Keep in mind that most people respect the fact that you are able to communicate in a second language. They want you to succeed.

Advance Preparation

These ongoing actions help non-native speakers of English master the language more quickly and thoroughly.

- *Immerse yourself in English.* Listen to English radio stations, and engage in English conversation whenever possible.

- *Learn phonetics.* You will learn how to make the sounds used in English that are not used in your native language and how to listen with greater comprehension.

- *Learn the American intonation pattern.* This pattern stresses nouns and verbs, as in "*Go* to the *office* and *check* the *file*." Listen to the difference between this pattern and other patterns that may be more flat or staccato.

- *Make a list of words that are difficult to pronounce.* Consciously note what makes each word difficult for you. Is it an unfamiliar consonant sound or stress on a particular syllable? Practice the words with a native speaker.

- *Record your own speech or review your voice-mail messages.* Listen, monitor, and practice your pronunciation.

Before Your Presentation

Practice with a friend or advisor who is a native speaker. Identify any challenges, then practice and polish as needed.

When Presenting

At your presentation, these actions help you be understood.

- *Face your listeners and make eye contact.* Maintain eye contact to help you judge whether they understand you.

- *Use natural facial expressions and gestures.* Facial expressions and other nonverbal clues increase the listeners' ability to understand.

Those English and Scottish know how to do accents.
JOEY MCINTYRE

- *Slow your rate of speech.* This will give your listeners a chance to become accustomed to your accent and speech patterns to distinguish between individual words. Invite your listeners to tell you if you speak too rapidly.

- *Pause if you need time to think.* Listeners are willing to wait. The pause will give them time to consider and process the information you have already covered.

- *If appropriate (and it often is), smile frequently while you speak.* It relaxes you. It relaxes your voice. It also relaxes your listeners and helps create a comfortable atmosphere where a lack of understanding can be acknowledged and overcome.

Best Practices for Native Speakers with Nonnatives

If English is your native language, the tips below will help you communicate effectively with nonnatives when making a presentation or participating in meetings or everyday conversations. As you use them, be sensitive to the fact that different listeners will likely have varied levels of expertise in English.

- *Face your listeners when speaking; face the speaker when you listen.* Your facial expressions and other nonverbal clues will increase the listeners' ability to understand you. You will be better able to judge whether they understand you.

- *Observe closely and check for understanding.* Be willing to stop and explain in a different way so that you maximize your ability to be understood without seeming to patronize your listeners.

- *Summarize early and often.* Whether you are making a presentation or participating in a meeting or conversation, this will help you identify barriers to good communication before they cause more problems.

- *Invite and encourage your listeners to ask for clarification.* Nonnative speakers may be reluctant to ask. Inviting them to do so can help put them at ease and create a more comfortable and cooperative atmosphere.

- *Slow your pace.* Give your listeners a chance to identify individual words and to ask for clarification when needed.

- *Invite your listeners to tell you if you speak too rapidly.* Again, nonnative speakers may be reluctant to tell you. Inviting them to do so can put them at ease and create a more comfortable and cooperative atmosphere.

- *If you don't understand what is said, ask the nonnative speaker to repeat it.* If that doesn't help, ask to see the word in writing. Then say the word out loud. The nonnative speaker will be able to hear it pronounced correctly.

- *Minimize slang and jargon.* Many such words and phrases are puzzling and easily misunderstood.

- *Limit humor, sarcasm, and word play.* These are often dependent on culture and can cause serious misunderstanding, confusion, or alienation.

- *Keep your sentences short and direct.* Avoid complex or rambling sentence structures. (You may want to avoid these with native speakers, also.)

- *Avoid thinking out loud.* Stay focused on one idea until you have finished it. Then make a clear transition to the next. Pause between ideas to allow the listeners to process information.

Summary

Preparation, practice, and the ongoing awareness that Web presentations present additional challenges for you and your listeners will help you succeed.

Delegating responsibilities, designing for interaction, and becoming familiar with the tools you will use will help you deliver effective Web presentations.

The rise of the global economy presents both challenges and the opportunity to give presentations to people of other languages and cultures. Familiarity with the correct pronunciation of words and the use of idioms will help you succeed in multi-lingual situations.

15

It's better to look ahead and prepare than to look back and regret.

JACKIE JOYNER-KERSEE

PREPARATION PRECEDES PERFECTION

The Polished Presentation Checklist

Planning reduces anxiety. It prevents the preventable problems.

Some problems can't be anticipated. Good planning will give you the time and clarity of mind to deal with surprises quickly, graciously, and with a sense of humor.

The speaker's checklist of essential information that follows will help you remember the details. Complete it to have the best chance of having everything you need when and where you need it.

To the left of each item is a box to check. You may want to photocopy this list to use whenever you need it. Give any assistant a copy of the list. Then agree on who will do what. This prevents "I thought *you* were going to do that!" just before your presentation.

Getting to the Venue

To reduce unnecessary stress, have the following information available.

❑ The venue's address, with detailed directions.

❑ All needed travel reservations with confirmation numbers.

❑ Confirmation of the delivery of materials sent in advance.

❑ Location of your materials, and name and phone number of person holding them.

❑ Phone number for help with delayed or canceled flights.

❑ Where to park and where to enter the building.

❑ The name and phone number of the person who will greet you.

❑ The names and phone numbers of at least two other people who could help you, for example, assistants, secretaries, building security personnel, concierge.

❑ If arriving outside of normal business hours, get an after-hours phone number.

❑ The name and location of the room where you will present your talk.

Hotel or Conference Center Information

Communicate early and often with the hotel or conference center staff. Their job is to give you what you need to succeed. They appreciate clear directions—they don't want last-minute emergencies any more than you do. The staff will be knowledgeable about the facilities. They know if a room can become too hot or cold, the best choices from their kitchen's menu, and other helpful details. Use their expertise when making arrangements. Make sure you get the following information:

❑ Confirmation of all pricing and payment agreements.

❑ Names and phone numbers of support staff: hotel managers, catering manager, audiovisual support, etc.

❑ List of services provided by both facility staff and contractors.

❑ If contractors are used, make sure they will be available when you need them, such as early in the morning to set up your equipment.

Seating Arrangements and Other Requirements

❑ Send the facility the specifics (a diagram is helpful) of your requirements.

❑ Confirm instructions were received, but don't trust that they were followed.

❏ Arrive early to check that the facility is set up the way you need it.

❏ Type of seating/number of seats.

❏ Tables/table arrangements.

❏ Space required in front of room.

❏ Lecterns or tables needed.

❏ Podium (raised speaking platform) with size requirements.

❏ Lighting requirements.

❏ Audiovisual requirements: microphones, projectors, screens, teleprompter, etc.

❏ Type and quantity of refreshments to be served.

❏ Specifics on the placement and timing of refreshment services.

These extra details are usually worth asking about. The venue staff should have the answers but probably won't mention them unless you ask.

❏ Where and when will the staff post the information about your presentation?

❏ What types of events are scheduled in adjoining rooms? How noisy will they be?

❏ Are adequate restroom facilities available?

❏ Will people in nearby rooms take breaks when you do? Can breaks be staggered?

❏ How quickly can the room be filled with and emptied of people?

❏ Is the screen the right size and in the right place? Should there be more than one?

❏ Does the room have temperature or ventilation issues? How are they dealt with?

❏ Will your refreshments be served on time? Quietly?

❑ If set up in a common area, will refreshments be safe from hungry "predators"?

❑ If you have bar service before your presentation, will it end before you begin?

Finally, what other details must be handled? What other information do you need to gather? What do you need to communicate to others? Make a list. Check off each item when it is done.

Summary

Plan thoroughly to minimize anxiety. Thorough preparation prevents problems. It will help you deal calmly and effectively with any unforeseeable problems. Use the above checklist to make sure that you arrive at the venue with time to spare and that the facility is appropriate for your needs and ready when you arrive.

EPILOGUE

The reduction of anxiety and the increase in confidence that come with truly understanding the body's natural response to public speaking—starts with understanding and accepting our human nature.

Most of us will never be able to eliminate our natural tendency to experience some nervousness when speaking to a group. But with the wisdom that comes with understanding that this anxiety is natural and normal, we can minimize it, prepare for it, and work with it to our advantage. We can feed our wolf, defeat our NME, and become excellent speakers in spite of it.

We can change. We can grow. To remain true to ourselves and reach our full potential, we must.

Enjoy your presentations, and enjoy the rewards they bring.

GLOSSARY

active voice A grammatical structure in which the subject of the verb performs the action, for example, "The speaker walked across the stage." This focuses attention on the subject. *See also* passive voice.

ad hominem Latin for "to the man." An error in logic that occurs when a speaker responds to an argument with a comment about the person making the opposing argument, not the merits of the argument itself. Positive or negative, the comment is usually irrelevant to the argument.

adrenal glands Two small endocrine glands, one located above each kidney, consisting of the cortex, which secretes several steroid hormones, and the medulla, which secretes adrenaline.

adrenaline A hormone produced by the body and released into the bloodstream in response to physical danger or mental stress. It starts many bodily responses that help the body cope with emergencies. Among other things, it stimulates heart action to increase the body's oxygen supply and increases blood sugar levels to provide extra energy.

analogy A comparison made to show some similarity between two things. Analogies can be used to infer that if things agree in some respects, they probably agree in others.

analyze To separate into essential parts and examine or interpret each part.

anxiety Concern, restlessness, and agitation about some thing or event. Anxiety is the result of a future vague, uncertain, or ill-defined threat.

appeal to authority An error in logic made by arguing that something is true because an authority says so, not because the argument has merit.

appeal to fear An error in logic made by using a threat of harm to advance one's position. The appeal to fear is also known as the argument from adverse consequences or swinging the big stick.

appeal to ignorance An error in logic made by assuming that something that has not been proved false must be true and vice versa.

argument from adverse consequences An error in logic made by using a threat of harm to advance the speaker's position. The argument from adverse consequences is also known as the appeal to fear or swinging the big stick.

autonomic nervous system That part of the nervous system that regulates basic involuntary functions of the body, including the activity of the heart and the smooth muscles, the muscles of the intestinal tract, and the glands.

begging the question Also known as assuming the answer or circular reasoning, this error in logic is made when an argument uses the proposition to prove itself. It may sound as if the speaker is giving a reason for something when he or she is simply restating it using different words.

body language Facial expressions, gestures, postures, movement, and proximity to others by which one communicates nonverbally.

cliché A phrase that was originally effective and vivid but has become trite or banal through overuse.

compare To examine two or more things in order to identify similarities and differences.

conclude To end or close, including a summary, result, inference, or decision.

contrast To set in opposition in order to show differences. Also, the visual effect of the juxtaposition of different colors, shades, or tones.

cortisol A hormone produced principally in response to physical or psychological stress and secreted by the adrenal glands.

criticize To make judgments about merits and faults. Criticism often accompanies analysis.

define To state the meaning of, to explain the essential qualities or nature of, to determine the precise limits of.

describe To convey an image or impression with words that reveals the appearance or nature of; to give an account of; to list parts, qualities, and characteristics of.

dialogue A conversation or interaction between two or more people intent on gaining insight or learning from one another.

diaphragmatic breathing A method of breathing more slowly and deeply than we tend to do when anxious. It helps us use the diaphragm correctly to expend less effort and energy to breathe. It can reduce many of the physical symptoms of anxiety.

discuss To examine by argument, consider and debate the pros and cons of an issue, explain conflicts; discussion often includes analysis, criticism, and comparison.

entrainment The synchronization of vibrations and behaviors that results in one body influencing and being influenced by another.

enumerate To list several things: ideas, aspects, events, qualities, reasons, and so on; to mention separately.

evaluate To appraise carefully, to determine the value or amount of.

excluded middle An error in logic made when one presents only two options, usually extremes, when more options exist. It implies that other options or compromise solutions are not possible. Also called false dilemma and false dichotomy.

explain To make clear and understandable, to make clear the cause or reason, to assign a meaning or interpret.

expound To give a methodical, detailed, scholarly explanation.

extemporaneous Given (as an unmemorized speech or presentation) from notes or an outline.

fallacy An argument that sounds convincing but is essentially flawed. Fallacies are errors in logic usually born from an attempt to persuade through nonlogical means. They can also be caused by careless thinking.

fallacy of popularity An error in logic that occurs when it is argued that something is true because it is believed to be true by so many people rather than because it has merit.

false analogy An error in logic made by using an argument that compares two very different things, states or implies that they are similar, and draws a conclusion about one based on the other. It becomes confusing when the two things are in some way similar; recognizing the flaw in the argument depends on seeing the differences clearly.

false dichotomy An error in logic made by using an argument that presents only two options, usually extremes, when more options exist. It implies that other options or compromise solutions are not possible. Also called the excluded middle and false dilemma.

false dilemma An error in logic made by using an argument that presents only two options, usually extremes, when more options exist. It implies that other options or compromise solutions are not possible. Also called excluded middle and false dichotomy.

fear An emotion of alarm and agitation caused by the anticipation, expectation, or realization of some specific pain or danger. Fear is usually accompanied by a desire to fight or flee.

fight-or-flight response The reaction and collective changes that occur in the body when faced by a sudden, unexpected threat or source of stress. The physical changes of the fight-or-flight response include a sharpening of the senses to help us detect and avoid physical dangers. They also give us increased physical strength and speed to fight or flee if the danger can't be avoided.

germane Vital to understanding. An element is germane if it cannot be removed without reducing comprehension.

grounding The processes by which we let our dialogue partners know how we have understood their messages—what we think they mean—and by which we seek evidence from them that our messages have been understood the way we meant them.

hasty generalization An error in logic made by generalizing using a sample that is too small to be conclusive. Also known as jumping to a conclusion.

illustrate To explain by giving examples or making comparisons.

impromptu Given (as a speech or presentation) without preparation and at a moment's notice.

inclusive language Language that avoids false assumptions about people regardless of their gender, marital status, ethnicity, disability, and age.

innate Inborn, native, natural. Not acquired by learning or conditioning.

interpret To explain, construe, or understand in a certain way; to give the meaning of something by paraphrase.

lexical gesture A gesture that helps the speaker remember a word or words.

loaded question A question that includes an assumption as an attempt to damage the position of the other party. This sidetracks the argument and can antagonize others by making them feel manipulated or bullied.

melatonin In animals, including humans, a hormone that anticipates the onset of darkness by generating the physical changes that lead to sleep.

metaphor A figure of speech that identifies one object or idea with another in one or more ways, for example, "The tiger's eyes were burning coals." Metaphors are used to suggest a similarity. *See also* simile.

monologue A speech or utterance by one person, usually at least several sentences long. Monologues often discourage others from participating in a conversation.

non sequitur Latin for "it doesn't follow." A non sequitur is an error in logic made when the conclusion of an argument fails to follow from its premise or premises.

nonverbal delivery skills Prosody and used as part of the delivery of information in a presentation or speech.

nonvocal paralanguage Body language. Variations in posture, gestures, facial expressions, and eye contact patterns are all nonvocal paralanguage. Examples include slumping, waving, smiling, and batting the eyes.

outline To give a general account or report including only the main points or features.

paralanguage Communication apart from the verbal communication of a message. Paralanguage changes or supplements the meaning of language. Gestures and tone of voice are examples of paralanguage.

parasympathetic nervous system That part of the autonomic nervous system which slows the heart rate, increases intestinal and gland activity, and so initiates the end of the fight-or-flight response.

passive voice A grammatical structure in which the subject of the verb receives the action, for example, "The winning point was made by the guard." Passive voice should be used when the action itself is more important than the person, persons, or thing that is acting. *See also* active voice.

phobia A persistent and seemingly irrational fear of a specific object, activity, or situation that results in a strong fear of and a desire to avoid it.

positive language Word choices and grammatical structures that communicate optimism and an expectation of the positive.

post hoc, ergo propter hoc An error in logic made by one assuming that because something happened after something else, it was caused by that thing. Latin for "it happened after, so it was caused by," it is often referred to as simply post hoc.

prejudicial language The error in logic made by using value-laden language. The use of prejudicial language states or implies that ethical or moral goodness is associated with agreeing with the argument. It often uses emotional or value-laden terms to accomplish this.

prosody The qualities of voice and vocal delivery that change the meaning of the verbal communication used. Volume, inflection, tone, rhythm, and pacing are examples of prosody. Humor and sarcasm are largely dependent on prosody.

prove To establish the truth or genuineness of by evidence or argument.

psychographics The study of the attitudes, values, belief systems, and ideologies of an individual, group, or culture.

rate To estimate quality or value, assign to a classification, or assign comparative worth.

red herring An error in logic made when something is said that sounds like it is relevant to the question or topic being discussed but is actually irrelevant. It can throw listeners off track, confuse the issue, and make it harder to reach an agreement and a conclusion.

redundancy The use of more words than necessary; that part of a message that can be eliminated without loss of essential information.

rhetorical question A question asked to encourage thought rather than elicit an answer. Rhetorical questions are often used to express an opinion or to emphasize a point.

salient object A thing having a quality that thrusts itself into attention; the center of attention or focus.

simile A figure of speech that expresses a resemblance between two things usually using the words like, as, or than, for example, "The tiger's eyes shone like burning coals." *See also* metaphor.

slippery slope An error in logic made by arguing that if a first step is taken, a disastrous and inevitable set of consequences will follow. These consequences are presented as the reason for not taking the first step. The slippery slope assumes an inability to make exceptions, set limits, or make decisions on a case-by-case basis.

straw man An error in logic committed when a speaker attacks an argument different from and weaker than the opposition's best argument. This is often done by caricaturing the opposition as so extreme in his views as to be ridiculous.

summarize To briefly and concisely state or restate main points.

swinging the big stick An argument in which the threat of harm is used to advance the speaker's position. Swinging the big stick is more formally known as the argument from adverse consequences or the appeal to fear.

sympathetic nervous system That part of the autonomic nervous system which accelerates the heart rate, constricts blood vessels, and raises blood pressure, and initiates the changes that result in the symptoms of the fight-or-flight response.

testosterone A steroid hormone and the most potent naturally occurring androgen that governs secondary sexual characteristics and may be positively correlated with confidence and aggression.

trace To follow the course, development, or history of; to show the order of events or progress of a subject or event.

transition A verbal device used to move from one section of a presentation to the next.

unrepresentative sample An error in logic that occurs when the sample used, even if quite large, is not representative of the population as a whole.

vocal paralanguage Utterances that can be heard but can't be found in the dictionary. Laughter, crying, sighing, grunting, snorting, and giggling are all examples of vocal paralanguage.

wrong-way street An error in logic that occurs when cause and effect are confused, that is, when an effect is assumed to be a cause or the cause is assumed to be an effect. This often happens because of limited perspective.

ABOUT THE AUTHOR

Mary Fensholt Perera is a business presentation consultant, coach, and award-winning author. She works with business and nonprofit executives, and professionals in sales, marketing, science, and technology, to improve their ability to present information in a confident, trustworthy, clear, and memorable way. And have fun doing it!

She has trained speakers for many internationally known companies, including Apple, AT&T, BAE Systems, Bank of America, Charles Schwab, Cisco Systems, Coca-Cola, Dell Computer, Edward D. Jones, Fluor, Hewlett-Packard, IBM, Intel, Incyte Genomics, Johnson & Johnson, KPMG, Merrill Lynch, Oracle, PricewaterhouseCoopers, Qualcomm, Silicon Genetics, and State Farm Insurance. Mary is a member of the faculty of the University of California at San Diego's Executive Perspectives for Scientists and Engineers and a frequent speaker for Vistage, an international organization of CEOs. She accepts additional training and speaking engagements on request.

The first edition of *The Polished Presentation,* published under the title *The Francis Effect,* won a Benjamin Franklin Award as one of the best psychology/self-help books of the year.

Educated at the University of Kansas and UCLA, she earned both a BA and MA in Communication Studies, graduated with distinction, and was selected to Phi Beta Kappa. She and her family enjoy traveling, biking, snow skiing, gardening, music, and the theater. She serves on the Board of Trustees of the Rancho Santa Ana Botanic Garden, and lives in Los Angeles, California.

INDEX

clichés, 69-71

closed questions, 157

closing the presentation, 58-61, 142

clothing. *See* dress/ appearance

Cohen, Ted, 99

Collins, Frederick L., 29

Collins, William, 180

color
    contrast, 106
    in visual aids, 106-107
    vision deficiency, 107

common ground, finding, 165

compare-and-contrast structure, 47

comparative images, 87
    clustering of, 90

comparisons, 52, 87

complexity, explaining, 88, 92, 95, 112

confidential information, 167

connecting with the audience, 16, 55, 114, 126, 146, 151

content,
    choosing a structure, 51-52
    developing notes, 42-43
    getting started, 41-42
    levels of preparation, 40-41
    memorizing, 13, 41, 139
    nonverbal, 123—124
    of answers, 167-169

controlling questioners, 168

coping self-statements, 21

cortisol, 10, 24, 105, 150

credibility,
    apologizing to audience and, 56
    consistency of verbal/ non-verbal messages and, 124, 170
    dress and appearance and, 116
    introductions and, 55-56
    questions and answers and, 161-163
    quotations and establishing, 101
    speaker's, with audience, 30-31,
    using speaker's in closing, 59

Cuddy, Amy, 24

Curry, Dell, 114

Curry, Stephen, 114

customers (audience), 34

D

Davis, Wade, 89-90

defensive behaviors, 128, 170

delivery skills (Web presentations), 186

demographics, 30-32

destination checks, 57

detail, level of, 33, 35, 53

Deutscher, Guy, 88, 92-93

dialogue(s),
    beginning with audience, 154-155
    connecting through, 111-113
    creating look and feel, 21, 126-127, 131-150, 152
    Engage-by-Stage four-stage model, 156-160
    purpose of 13-15, 18
    versus monologue, 11-13
    with audience, 18,161

diaphragmatic breathing, 22-23

disconnection from audience, 13-16

diverse audiences, 34-35, 101, 187-191

Dostoyevsky, Fyodor, 35

Doudna, Jennifer, 89

dress/appearance
    business attire, 115-118
    business casual, 116
    grooming, 117
    knowing your goal for, 115-116
    overall appearance, 115

dry mouth, 7, 9

Dumbledore, Albus, 141

Dunbar, Robin, 151

E

eating smart, 20

editing the presentation, 62-63

Effective Communication Skills for Scientific and Technical Professionals (Chambers), 168-169,

emojis, 14

emoticons, 14

ending question-and-answer sessions, 171

end users (audience) 34

Engage-by-Stage four-stage model, 156-160

Englebert, Omer, 17

English as a second language, issues of, 181, 188-189

entrainment, 15-16

Erwitt, Elliot, 103

evolutionary response to danger. *See* also fight-or-flight response

examples, using, 37, 48, 52

executives
    as audience, 33-34
    answering questions from, 169-170

exercise, 20, 23-24

experts (audience), 33-34

extemporaneous delivery, 40-41

eye contact,
    confidence and, 126
    controlling questioners and, 168
    guidelines for effective, 126
    honesty and, 126
    hostile questioners and, 168
    notes and, 140
    observing listener's and, 123
    questions and answers and, 164, 170-171
    teleprompters and, 148
    video presentations and, 187
    visual aids and, 140-141

F

facial expressions, 130-131, 170

fallacies, logical, 173-180

false analogy fallacy, 178

familiar information, 82-84, 87-88

Fancy or Strong word list, 66

FAQs (frequently asked questions), 162

fear. *See* anxiety

fight or flight, 131-150,152

filtering information, 81

fonts/typefaces for slides, 107-108

Forster, E.M., 90

Fowler, W., 64

framing answers, 167-169

Francis and the Wolf, 17-18

Frank, Robert, 112

frequently misused words, 76-79

Freud, Sigmund, 93

Frost, Robert, 82, 181

G

gather and group approach, 43

gathering information, group and gather approach, 49

gender-neutral language, 73-75

general-to-specific structure, 45

geographic structure, 45

NOTES

1   James Trefil, *Are We Unique? A Scientist Explores the Unparalleled Intelligence of the Human Mind* (John Wiley & Sons, Inc., 1997), 21-22.

2   Edward O. Wilson, *On Human Nature* (Cambridge, MA: Harvard University Press, 1978), 68.

3   Stress: Fight or Flight Response, Psychologist World, Psychologist World and Partners, 2006. https://www.psychologistworld.com/stress/fightflight.php. (accessed June 22, 2016).

4   Matt Ridley, *Nature Via Nurture* (New York, HarperCollins, 2003), 192-195.

5   Fried and Hademenos, *Theories and Problems of Biology*, 230.

6   Alison Tekeda, "What Makes Hair Stand On End When You're Scared?" Emotional Health, 10/28/11, http://www.everydayhealth.com/emotional-health/what-makes-hair-stand-on-end-when-youre-scared.aspx (accessed June 24, 2016).

7   Elaine Morgan, *The Scars of Evolution* (Oxford, England: Oxford University Press, 1994), 85-87.

8   John D. MacArthur, "The Human Brain: How Your Brain Responds to Stress," Franklin Institute Online, http://www.fi.edu/brain/stress.htm (accessed August 15, 2004).

9   Clayton, Martin, Sager, Rebecca and Will, Udo, "In time with the music: The concept of entrainment and its significance for musicology," final draft before publication, available online at http://perso.wanadoo.fr/esem/ECP_WEB/Articles/Vol. 1/IYWTM.htm (accessed June 24, 2006).

10 Ibid., 22-23.

11 John Shea, *Starlight* (New York: Crossroad Publishing Company, 1996), 47-51.

12 Omer Englebert, *St. Francis of Assisi: A Biography* (Cincinnati, Ohio: Servant Books, 2013).

13 "Beyond Hangovers: understanding alcohol's impact on your health," National Institute of Health publication, http://pubs.niaaa.nih.gov/publications/Hangovers/beyondangovers.pdf (accessed September 24, 2016).

14 Kris Gunnars, BSC, "10 Disturbing Reasons Why Sugar Is Bad For You," https:// authoritynutrition.com/10-disturbing-reasons-why-sugar-is-bad/ (accessed September 23, 2016).

15 Sophia Breene, "13 Mental Health Benefits of Exercise," Huffington Post, http:// www.huffingtonpost.com/2013/03/27/mental-health-benefits-exercise (accessed September 20, 2016).

16 For more insights into the soothing power of walking see Chatwin, Bruce, *The Songlines*, 229, 230.

17 Amy Cuddy, "Your body language shapes who you are," TED, 2012. http://www.ted. com/talks/amy_cuddy_your_body_language_shapes_who_you_are?language=en (accessed August 24, 2016).

18 "Definition of Beta blocker," MedicineNet.com, http://www.medicinenet.com/ script/main/art.asp?articlekey=2452 (accessed September 24, 2016).

19 Aaron Taube "Here's The Pill That Could Make Your Next Big Presentation A Hit," Business Insider, http://www.businessinsider.com/pill-can-make-next-presentation-a-hit-2014-8 (accessed September 24, 2016).

20 Robert Palmer, "The Panama Papers Exposed a Huge Global Problem. What's Next?" Panahttps://www.ted.com/talks/robert_palmer_the_panama_papers_exposed_a_huge_global_problem_what_s_next?language=en (accessed June 13, 2016).

21 Jeff Haden, "10 Stupid Phrases the Worst Bosses Love to Use," Inc., July 6th, 2015. http://www.inc.com/jeff-haden/10-stupid-phrases-the-worst-bosses-love-to-use. html. (accessed June 19, 2016).

22 Tom Leblanco and Manu Raju, "Kasich apologizes for saying women 'left their kitchens' to back him," CNN Politics, February 22, 2016.
http://www.cnn.com/2016/02/22/politics/john-kasich-women-kitchen/ (accessed June 25, 2016).

23 Gretchen McCulloch, 2015 Word of the Year is singular "they" American Dialect Society, All Things Linguistic, January, 2016. http://allthingslinguistic.com/post/ 136976055258/2015-word-of-the-year-is-singular-they (accessed June 25, 2016).

24 Bill Jensen, *Simplicity* (Cambridge, MA: Perseus Publishing, 2001).

25 J. L. McGaugh, "Significance and Remembrance: the Role of Neuromodulatory Systems," Psychological Science I (1990): 15-25.

26 Michael Kinsley, "Please Don't Quote Me," Time, May 13, 1991, 82.

27 Russell Ash, *Incredible Comparisons* (New York: DK Publishing, Inc. 1996), 23.

28 Ibid.,15.

29 Guy Deutscher, PhD, *The Unfolding of Language* (New York: Picador, 2005), 142.

30 "Words That Resonate," The Healing Spectrum, http://www.thehealingspectrum. com/quotes.html (accessed December 3, 2004).

31 Paula Hammond, PhD, "A new superweapon in the fight against cancer," TED talks live, November, 2015. http://www.ted.com/talks/paula_hammond_a_new_ superweapon_in_the_fight_against_cancer/transcript?language=en#t-260914 (accessed September 25, 2016).

32 Jennifer Doudna, PhD, "How CRISPR Lets Us Edit Our DNA," TED Global, London, 2015, https://www.ted.com/talks/jennifer_doudna_we_can_now_ edit_our_dna_but_let_s_do_it_wisely?language=en (accessed May 3rd, 2016).

33 Wade Davis, "Dreams From Endangered Cultures" TED 2003, February, 2003, https://www.ted.com/talks/wade_davis_on_endangered_cultures, (accessed May 30, 2016).

34 Guy Deutscher, PhD, *The Unfolding of Language* (New York: Picador, 2005), 143.

35 Guy Deutscher, PhD, *The Unfolding of Language* (New York: Picador, 2005), 143.

36 Annette Simmons, *The Story Factor* (Cambridge, MA: Perseus Publishing, 2001), 5.

37 Ibid., 4.

38 Egan Kieran, "Memory, Imagination and Learning: Connected by the Story," http:// www.educ.sfu.ca.kegan/Memorylm.html (accessed February 10, 2005).

39 David M. Armstrong, *Managing by Storying Around* (New York: Doubleday Currency, 1992).

40 Julie Fenster, *In the Words of Great Business Leaders* (New York: John Wiley & Sons, 2000), 137,138.

41 David Pogue, "Simplicity Sells," TED, 2006. https://www.ted.com/talks/ david_pogue_says_simplicity_sells/transcript?language=en

42 Jerry Rice, "Next Stop: Atlantis," Inland Valley, (CA) Daily Bulletin, Entertainment, 6, May 29, 2004.

43 Ted Cohen, *Jokes: Philosophical Thoughts on Joking Matters* (Chicago: The University of Chicago Press, 1999).

44 Edward O. Wilson, *Biophilia* (Cambridge, MA: Harvard University Press, 1984).

45 Color Blindness Prevalence in News-Medical.Net, Life Sciences and Medicine, Feb. 5th, 2014. (accessed January 5, 2016).

46 NOAH, May 11, 2016. http://www.noaa.gov/national-weather-service-will-stop-using-all-caps-its-forecasts (accessed May 11, 2016).

47 Lena Groegor, "How Typography Can save Your Life," ProPublica, May 11, 2016, https://www.propublica.org/article/how-typography-can-save-your-life (accessed March 11, 2016).

48 Visual message design and learning: The role of static and dynamic illustrations. In D.H. Jonassen (Ed.), *Handbook of Research for Educational Communications and Technology* (New York: Simon and Schuster Macmillan).

49 Edward R. Tufte, "PowerPoint Is Evil," Wired, September 2003.

50 Ethan Sherwood Strauss, "You won't believe how Nike lost Steph to Under Armour," ESPN, March 23, 2016, http://espn.gocom/nba/story/_/id/15047018/how-nike-lost-stephen-curr-armour (accessed June 27, 2016).

51 Philip Ball, "Loud Voices Music To Our Ears," Nature News Service, 2001, http://www.nature.com/nsu/010524/010524-2.html (accessed May 21, 2001).

52 Robert M. Krauss, Yihsiu Chen, and Rebecca F. Gottesman, "Lexical Gestures and Lexical Access: A Process Model," http:// www.columbia.edu/~rmk7/PDF/GSP.pdf (accessed June 27, 2016).

53 John Bowlby, *A Secure Base* (New York: Basic Books, 1988), 7-8.

54 Robin Dunbar, *Grooming, Gossip, and the Evolution of Language* (Cambridge, MA: Harvard University Press, 1997), 121.

55 Ronald P. Marks, "Improving On-line Sales Education," Learning Developer's Journal (October 1, 2002), http://www.elearningguild.com/pdf/2/100102des-1.pdf (accessed June 25, 2004).

56 Ben Woods, "By 2020, 90% of world's population over age 6 will have a mobile phone," The Next Web. http://thenextweb.com/insider/2014/11/18/2020-90-worlds-population-aged-6-will-mobile-phone-report/ (accessed June 25, 2016).

57 Gerald D. Fischback, *Mind and Brain: A Scientific American Special Report*, 1994, 8.

58 Bloomberg Politics, March 4, 2016. http://www.bloomberg.com/politics/trackers/2016-03-04/kasich-i-m-not-biting-on-whether-trump-is-naive-about-putin (accessed June 10, 2016).

59 Harry E. Chambers, *Effective Communication Skills for Scientific and Technical Professionals* (New York: Perseus Publishing, 2001), 125.

CPSIA information can be obtained
at www.ICGtesting.com
Printed in the USA
FSOW03n0259181117
41188FS